Contents

Introduction

Welcome to *Bright Ideas: Games for Building Social Skills*. This book offers a wide range of activities that link to the QCA Schemes of Work for citizenship at Key Stages 1 and 2.

The focus of the activities in this book is very firmly on learning through enjoyment. The children can reflect upon key areas in social skills and consider ways in which they can make positive differences in terms of their responses and interactions with others. Adult input is crucial for them to achieve success and should not be underestimated. Allowing the children to engage at their own level, while supporting them as a facilitator and friendly critic, will allow the children to grow emotionally and socially.

The themes covered in the book deliberately intertwine to allow the children to consistently reinforce key principles of quality communication and full participation with their peers. Many of the activities involve small-group or paired work. Once again, your input in observing the children's interactions and in supporting their individual development in social skills will assist in achieving these key principles.

Resourcing the activities
Many of the activities require few extra resources and can be conducted as integral parts of the core curriculum. Where resources are needed, these are largely limited to those commonly found in the classroom or are provided as photocopiable pages in the book.

The organisation of the book
The book covers six themes, reflecting key areas of citizenship at Key Stages 1 and 2.

● Sharing and taking turns
Board games are ideal activities to encourage children to share and to take turns. Some children have limited opportunities to play these games and their first opportunities may be presented at school. These children may find these activities challenging because they have to wait for their turn. However, other children respond positively to sharing and taking turns because the games provide a sense of order.

● Co-operation and collaboration
Key skills of co-operation and collaboration demand a great deal of effort from children. These skills require constant revisiting to allow the children to test out their own input and responses, and to learn ways of mastering effective communication with others. They learn how to achieve the results they want through positive interactions. Children need to be taught how to engage effectively and they need the opportunity to discover the benefits of interacting with others in a safe and supportive environment.

● Moral values
Through learning moral values – of knowing right from wrong – children are taught to understand the ramifications of their actions. Every action has a consequence – not only for the person who is undertaking the action, but also for everyone else involved. These activities highlight the emotional issues associated with making choices, and the decision wheel allows the children to consider the different choices available to them.

● Listening and speaking skills
Experience shows us that many children speak with ease, but listening may remain an enigma! Listening skills are essential for offering appropriate responses and communicating effectively.

● **Small group participation**
Group participation brings together many of the skills outlined above, and it relies on the ability of children to interact and communicate effectively. Games such as 'Give, Take or Swap' and 'Adders' rely heavily on the children's responses to each other. The teachers' input is important to encourage positive and supportive group behaviour.

● **Diversity**
These activities encourage children to explore issues associated with differences among people. The children are encouraged to consider their own and others' views about 'being different'. Differences should be regarded as positive, and children should be aware that all people could make positive contributions to society, irrespective of race, creed and disability.

Each activity is broken down into the following areas:

Age range
Although each game is targeted at children at the level specified, many of the activities can be extended with creativity and flexible management to cover the whole primary age range.

Learning objectives
Included on each page is a section that identifies the learning focus of the activity. The focus for the learning objectives is taken directly from the QCA citizenship guidance.

Curriculum links
This section specifies the clear, distinct links with the QCA Schemes of Work for citizenship at Key Stages 1 and 2 and the National Curriculum PSHE and citizenship guidelines.

What you need
The resources required to carry out the activities are listed in this section. For most games the resources are minimal. It may be helpful to allow the children to take increasing responsibility for the preparation of the activities and to allow them to organise resources whenever possible. This supports them in becoming active partners in preparing as well as implementing their educational activities.

What to do
Information for conducting each activity is presented in short bullet points. Experience has shown that it is most effective to 'digest' this information well in advance of presenting the activity to the children for the first time.

Differentiation
At the end of each activity there are ideas for extending the learning for more able children, and for supporting or adapting the activity for less able children. These suggest only a few examples and, once again, experience has shown that the children also bring their own creative ideas for further developmental work.

Photocopiable pages
Many of the activities use the photocopiable sheets included with this book. Some are used as gameboards, and it may be helpful to keep some as laminated copies for future use. The use of the photocopiable sheets is clearly detailed in the 'What to do' section.

CHAPTER 1

Sharing and taking turns

AGE RANGE 5–11

LEARNING OBJECTIVE
To take turns; to participate in speaking and listening; to learn to retain facts.

CURRICULUM LINKS
QCA citizenship, Unit 1: Taking part.

Treasure trove

What you need
A small box decorated as a treasure box, large enough for an item of treasure to fit inside; items that can be used as a treasure collection.

What to do
● This activity may be used with a whole class, large or small group.
● Ask for a volunteer to come to the front. Seat the rest of the class in a circle and give each child a number.
● Show the class the treasure box and explain that the volunteer is the treasure keeper. Move away from the circle and place one item of treasure in the box so that only you and the treasure keeper know what the treasure is. Then ask the treasure keeper to take the treasure box and sit in the middle of the circle.
● Starting with number 1, ask the children to call out their numbers in turn. The treasure keeper can call out *Stop!* at any point and ask that child: *What's in my treasure box?*
● The chosen child may ask one question about the treasure. They can then take a guess at what they think the treasure is, or choose to pass.
● The children can then resume calling out their numbers, starting with the child after the one who asked the last question.
● Reinforce the details given in the children's questions each time and the answers they receive. This will support the children in learning to retain facts, and will ensure the children continue to ask appropriate questions and provide realistic guesses.
● The child who guesses the item of treasure correctly becomes the treasure keeper, and the game can start again with a new item of treasure in the box.

Differentiation
For more able children, provide rules that make the game more challenging. For example, the children must discover the identity of the treasure within a certain number of questions. Less able children could design and make their own treasure boxes.

AGE RANGE 5–6

LEARNING OBJECTIVE
To participate in speaking and listening; to take turns.

CURRICULUM LINKS
QCA citizenship, Unit 1: Taking part.

Knowledge busters (1)

What you need
Sets of prepared questions to ask the children; paper and pencils.

What to do
● Before the lesson, prepare sets of simple questions on a range of categories. For example, on colour, nature, music, spelling, logic, shape (2-D or 3-D shapes), addition and subtraction or topic-related questions.

● Begin the lesson by discussing with the children what a quiz is. Talk about the process followed during a quiz. For example, a question is asked, an answer is given and a score is recorded. Reinforce the roles of each participant in a quiz and stress the importance of remaining quiet until it's their turn.
● Give the children some examples of quiz questions and invite individuals to answer them. For example, *How many sides does a triangle have? Which day comes before Saturday?*
● Tell the children they are going to take part in a class quiz. Divide the class into teams. Keep the teams small in number so the children do not have to wait too long for their turns.
● Using your prepared questions, ask the first team a set of questions.
● Give the teams that are watching paper and pencils to tally the number of correct answers that the team obtains.
● Continue until each team has answered a set of questions. The winners are the team that gets the most answers correct.
● There are opportunities to encourage the children to write their own questions and answers, but the primary focus is enhancing the children's speaking and listening skills.

Differentiation
Introduce basic rules to increase the complexity of the quiz for more able children. Ensure you set appropriate questions for less able children at the correct level. Alternatively, an adult could work with a group of less able children.

Games for Building Social Skills BRIGHT IDEAS

AGE RANGE 7–11

LEARNING OBJECTIVE
To participate as a team member; to ask and answer questions appropriately; to develop research skills.

CURRICULUM LINKS
QCA citizenship, Unit 1: Taking part.

Knowledge busters (2)

What you need
Reference books; Internet access; paper and pencils; a board and writing materials.

What to do
● Tell the children they are going to play a class quiz in teams. Explain that you want them to write their own questions and to agree their own rules for the quiz.
● Divide the class into teams and give each team a subject category. These should correspond to areas that the children are familiar with or they may link to a recent topic (for example, history, science, spelling, a chosen topic, mental maths).
● Give paper and pencils to each team and tell them that you want them to research an agreed number of quiz questions for their subject category. Emphasise the importance of pitching the questions correctly. They need to be challenging – some questions might be easier and some might be more difficult – but none should be too difficult. Give the teams reference books and Internet access, and let them conduct their research and write their questions.
● Ask the teams to agree basic rules for the quiz. These might include the amount of time allowed to answer each question, penalties, bonus points, the number of points for a correct answer or the number of points deducted for a wrong answer. Record the agreed rules on the board.
● When the teams are ready to start, arrange the furniture to adopt a formal quiz setting. Ask for a volunteer to be the quiz monarch who will ask the questions. Explain that now the quiz is starting the rest of the children are quizlings. This will help to reinforce the roles that the children are playing.
● The teams should give the quiz monarch their questions. Explain that two teams will play against each other, the quiz monarch asking them alternate questions. Give the onlooking teams pencils and paper and ask them to keep score. They can also ensure that the agreed rules are adhered to.
● At the end of the quiz announce the winning team and proclaim them the Knowledge busters.

Differentiation
For less able children, set questions yourself based on focused areas of work. More able children could challenge another class or year group to compete against them.

AGE RANGE 5–6

LEARNING OBJECTIVE
To take turns; to repeat and retain facts.

CURRICULUM LINKS
QCA citizenship, Unit 1: Taking part.

Have you seen...?

What you need
Paper; drawing and painting materials.

What to do
● Seat the children in a circle.
● Begin the game yourself with a question. For example, *Have you seen the orange cat with one tail?*
● Ask the child sitting next to you to repeat the question and add a detail about the cat. For example, *Have you seen the orange cat with one tail and two eyes?*
● Ask the next child to repeat the question and add another detail. For example, *Have you seen the orange cat with one tail, two eyes and three fleas?* The fourth child might say, *Have you seen the orange cat with one tail, two eyes, three fleas and four legs?*
● Invite the children to include funny details.
● Continue to take turns moving around the circle with the children, and adding more details until the list is too long to remember.
● Once the list is too long to remember, ask the child who was unable to remember the list to think of a new question.
● You may wish the children to draw pictures of the subject of the game. For instance, they could paint a picture of an orange cat with one tail, a red dog with four legs or a lorry with one aerial. These could be used as a bank to repeatedly begin this activity.

Differentiation
For those children who grasp the game quickly, introduce competition. Who can remember the most facts? For less able children, tell each child the fact they must memorise. Is each child able to retain this while building the list of facts?

Games for Building
Social Skills **BRIGHT IDEAS**

AGE RANGE 5–11

LEARNING OBJECTIVE
To listen and respond appropriately in a group.

CURRICULUM LINKS
QCA citizenship, Unit 1: Taking part.

Story sounds

What you need
A variety of musical instruments; photocopiable page 18; an acetate version of photocopiable page 18; an overhead projector.

What to do
● Let the children explore a small number of musical instruments (approximately four to six). Encourage them to create a wide variety of sounds by playing the instruments in different ways. For example: with a tambourine, using fingernails or the flat of the hand, shaking it hard or softly; with a triangle, playing with different types of beaters, using different materials to hit it; with bells, shaking them hard or softly, running fingers up and down the bells.

● Read one of the stories on photocopiable page 18 to the children.

● Put the acetate version of the story on to the overhead projector and re-read the story. Encourage the children to talk about the sounds that occur in the story and invite them to suggest which words might be used to introduce musical sounds. Explain that these sounds could be used to reinforce a mood, a word or a phrase. Highlight their suggestions in the text.

● Ask the children to suggest the instruments they believe will reflect the moods or words best and how the instruments should be played. For example, in 'Night ride' the children may wish to use coconut shells or a tambourine to represent the sound of the horses, or in 'Magic and mystery' shaking a tambourine gently so that the bells tinkle mysteriously when the ghost hunt is mentioned.

● Choose one member of the class to act as the storyteller. Ask the storyteller to read through the story again. Let the children introduce their musical sounds in the appropriate places. Encourage the children to work together and to decide who will play each sound effect.

● Encourage different storytellers to retell the story and let other children play the chosen instruments. Each time, ask how the children think they could improve their performance.

Differentiation
More able children can make up their own stories and add musical accompaniment to these. Less able children can be encouraged to create stories by working in a group of approximately four children. The group should agree on a story theme. The first child should make up the first few sentences of the story, then the next child continues, followed by the other members of the group until the story is completed. They can then add musical sounds to their story.

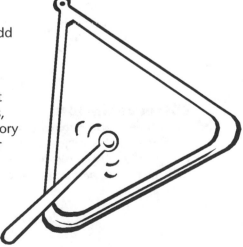

AGE RANGE 5–11

LEARNING OBJECTIVE
To encourage co-operation when working in pairs to produce a finished piece of art.

CURRICULUM LINKS
QCA citizenship, Unit 1: Taking part.

Collage for two

What you need
Card; pencils; collage materials; glue and glue sticks; scissors (enough for the children to work in pairs).

What to do
● Put the class into pairs and nominate each child as either child A or child B. Give each pair a piece of backing card, collage materials, glue and scissors. The primary objective of the activity is to encourage the children to work with each other. It is helpful, therefore, to have a restricted supply of collage materials. This will encourage the children to discuss the project in greater detail and to actually work together to achieve an end product.

● Tell the children you want them to make a collage in their pairs. Encourage them to discuss the subject for their collage with their partner.

● When they have agreed what their collage will be, ask them to draw an outline on to the card.

● Let the children begin their collages, deciding which materials they will use.

● After five or ten minutes, ask child B to move on to the next table to work with a new partner on their collage.

● Tell child A, who has remained *in situ*, to explain to their new partner the subject of the collage. They can then work together to create this.

● After a further five or ten minutes, ask child A to move on to the next table to work with child B to complete the collage on that table. This time, child B will remain with the collage to explain the content and process to their new partner.

● At the end of the lesson, ask the original pairs on each table to return to their original collage and discuss the finished article.

Differentiation
More able children may be provided with a subject or theme and asked to complete a collage on this subject. More restrictions might be introduced to increase the complexity of the project. Less able children may find it easier to undertake the whole collage in their pair and then to change partners to begin another piece of artwork.

AGE RANGE 5–11

LEARNING OBJECTIVE
To engage with others in playing a game; to take turns and use rules to support the process of a game; to learn to win and lose appropriately.

CURRICULUM LINKS
QCA citizenship, Unit 1: Taking part.

Weather warning

What you need
Card copies of the gameboard on photocopiable page 19; card copies of photocopiable page 20, the individual weather cards cut out; dice; coloured counters (enough of each resource for the children to work in groups of four).

What to do
● Before the lesson, write the rules of the game (outlined below) on the board.
● Put the class into groups of four. Tell the children they are going to play a game in their groups. Give them a set of weather cards from photocopiable page 20 and ask them to create their own weather cards on the blank ones. For example, they could draw a tornado.
● Give each group a board (photocopiable page 19), a die and counters. Then explain the rules of the game to the children.

1) They must start by placing their weather cards face down.
2) Each player takes it in turn to throw the die and move their counter along the board.
3) If a player throws a 2, 4 or 5 they must pick up a weather card. Some of the weather cards offer bonuses or penalties as follows:
   Sun = move on 2 spaces
   Lightning = move on 3 spaces
   Rain = move back 1 space
   Fog = miss a go.
4) If the children pick up any other weather card they move on 1 space.

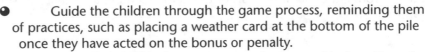

● Guide the children through the game process, reminding them of practices, such as placing a weather card at the bottom of the pile once they have acted on the bonus or penalty.
● Monitor the children's responses to winning and losing. How do they cope with being penalised? How do they manage being the winning group?
● Use these areas as discussion points with them after the game. Some children may find losing difficult, while others may gloat when winning. Discuss how the children could cope losing and how they can manage being a winner without hurting the losers' feelings. Encourage appropriate responses.

Differentiation
More able children may wish to create their own rules and write a guide on how to play the game. Some children will have limited experience of playing board games. It may be helpful to use an older, or more able, child to lead a small group initially. Reduce the numbers of penalties and bonuses to keep the game simple.

AGE RANGE 5–6

LEARNING OBJECTIVE
To use rules and take turns; to maintain concentration even though they may not constantly be the focus of attention; to interact appropriately with other children whilst playing a game (such as counting and moving counters, passing the die to their opponent appropriately).

CURRICULUM LINKS
QCA citizenship, Unit 1: Taking part.

Knights of old

What you need
Card copies of photocopiable page 21; dice; coloured counters (enough of each resource for the children to work in pairs).

What to do
● Put the class into pairs and give each pair a copy of photocopiable page 21. Tell them that they are going to play a game and that they can affect how it will be played.
● Ask the children to make the circles on the photocopiable sheet into faces. Explain that these should be a mixture of smiley and sad faces.
● Give each pair a die and counters. Explain to the children that the object of the game is to be the first player to reach the castle.
● Explain the rules to the children:

1) Each player throws the die and moves their counter along the board.
2) If a player lands on a square that has an arrow on it, they must follow the direction of the arrow on their next go.
3) If a player lands on a smiley face, they may move one square ahead.
4) If a player lands on a sad face, they must drop back a square and lose a go.
5) If a player overtakes their opponent, they have to swap counters. Player A would take player B's counter, and vice versa.

● The winner is the first player to reach the castle.
● It is helpful to write these rules on the board to ensure all the children understand and follow them.
● Let the children play the game. Invite them to discuss their experiences afterwards. Was the game easy to understand? Did they enjoy the game? Which were the easy or challenging parts? Is there anything that they would like to add to the game?

Differentiation
More able children can make up their own set of game rules. Less able children may benefit from either adult support or the help of a more able child to work through the game together.

Games for Building
Social Skills **BRIGHT IDEAS**

AGE RANGE 5–6

LEARNING OBJECTIVE
To recognise that actions have consequences and these can be both good and bad; to help children understand that they can make others feel good or bad by the way they act towards them.

CURRICULUM LINKS
QCA citizenship, Unit 1: Taking part.

You are invited

What you need
Copies of photocopiable page 22 (enough for one per child); pencils; coloured pencils and crayons; a board and writing materials.

What to do
● Tell the children you want them to imagine they are hosting a party. Ask them questions to start them thinking about their planning, such as: *Who are you going to invite? How many guests are you going to invite?*

● Give each child a copy of photocopiable page 22 and tell them that this is their party invitation. They need to send this to their guests. Go through the invitation with the class and make sure they know what details they need to fill in.

● Let the children fill in their invitation. They can colour it and add other illustrations.

● The activity may consist of this simple lesson-length activity, or could be extended over a number of lessons to reinforce aspects of social interaction. This may include listing games the children would like to play at the party, making decisions about what the party game prizes will be, whether there will be party bags or party hats, and so on.

● Use this as an opportunity to discuss feelings with the children and to make them see that what they do has an effect on others. Ask how it feels to be invited to a party. Ask the children how they would feel if they were not invited to a party. Point out that by sending or not sending invitations to friends they can influence how their friends feel.

● Encourage the children to use verbal interaction with each other by letting them role-play party scenarios using appropriate language. For example, inviting someone to a party and responding to an invitation appropriately, congratulating the winner of a party game and commiserating with a loser. Teach the children the appropriate skills to use when inviting or accepting (or declining) an invitation, and encourage the children to lose and win appropriately.

Differentiation
Encourage more able children to role-play the part of inviting peers to their party and presenting them with the invitation. Less able children may find writing the invitation a challenge, so provide them with templates of key words. Have an adult on hand to write the content for them so the children can copy this out.

AGE RANGE 7–11

LEARNING OBJECTIVE
To use pictures as a source of inspiration; to discuss the content and to create with others sound 'pictures' that reflect the picture's content.

CURRICULUM LINKS
QCA citizenship, Unit 1: Taking part.

Sound pictures

What you need

A picture that can be interpreted in sound, such as a brightly coloured poster, a computer screen saver (sea pictures or cloud formations); your own choice of picture and a short piece of music that reflects it; a variety of tuned musical instruments, such as xylophones, glockenspiels, chime bars, hand bells, a variety of beaters; a tape recorder; blank cassettes.

What to do

● Show the children your own choice of picture and play the piece of music that you feel reflects its mood. Talk about how the picture makes you feel and why you think the music reflects this, emphasising the use of adjectives.

● Show the children the picture that they are going to use. Invite them to look at it carefully and to employ adjectives to describe how the picture makes them feel.

● Ask key questions to prompt the children, such as: *Does the picture convey a mood to you? How does the picture make you feel? Would you like to go there? Why?*

● Put the children into groups of four to six. Explain that they are going to create a musical 'picture' that describes the mood and feel of the picture.

● Encourage the groups to think of the musical picture they are going to create in three sections: the beginning, middle and end.

● Allow the children to experiment with the musical instruments, experiencing the variety of pitch and dynamics that each is capable of making.

● Give the groups time to practise and refine their musical picture. When they are ready, tape-record each group's musical picture and play these to the rest of the class.

Differentiation

More able children may benefit from working together. Let them experiment with written notation to capture their musical piece in written form. Less able children may need support when discussing the picture's content. Give adult guidance to ensure the children choose appropriate instruments and also play them properly.

AGE RANGE 5–11

LEARNING OBJECTIVE
To encourage appropriate responses to game rules
(including taking and missing turns).

CURRICULUM LINKS
QCA citizenship, Unit 1: Taking part.

Go for it!

What you need
Card copies of the gameboard on photocopiable page 19 (enough for the children to work in pairs); 6cm by 6cm blank cards (enough for six cards per child); a board and writing materials; dice; coloured counters.

What to do
● Give each child a set of six blank cards and some coloured pencils. Ask them to mark two of their cards with a large cross (X), two with a plus sign (+) and two with a minus sign (–).
● Explain to the children that they are going to use these cards in a board game. Write up on the board what the cards signify:

1) The X card means players miss a go.
2) The + card means players may move on two spaces.
3) The – card means players must move back. They must throw a die to decide how many spaces they go back.

● Put the class into pairs and give each pair a gameboard (photocopiable page 19), a die and two coloured counters. Explain the rules of the game to the children.
● The game relies on strategy and a cool head! The players need to strategically use their cards to their best advantage at chosen points in the game.
● To start the game, the die is thrown by each player in turn. The player who throws the highest number goes first.
● The players take it in turns to throw the die and move along the board.
● They must use their cards to help them be the first to reach the finish. As they progress through the game, each player can put one of their cards on the gameboard before their opponent moves their counter. Their opponent must then act on the instruction on the card. For example, if player A puts down a 'X' card, player B must miss a go.
● Players can only use each of their cards once and they have to use up all of their cards by the end of the game.
● The player who successfully reaches the final square is the winner.

Differentiation
More able children can make up further rules to increase the complexity of the game. Use a larger board and increase the number of players to four to challenge them. Less able children may need help to learn how to play the game strategically and use their game cards at the best time.

Story sounds

Night ride

Was it a dream or was it real? Monique wasn't sure. But there they were, proudly lifting their white heads as they rounded the corner of the elegant castle. Six pure dazzling white horses. Behind them the carriage glittered in the full sunlight. This magnificent sight could have belonged to Cinderella herself.

   It was only as the carriage drew level and slowed that Monique was able to see inside the small, diamond-shaped windows. She recoiled in horror. How could such an ugly hag, with straggly grey streaked hair and evil piercing eyes, ride in such beauty and splendour?

Magic and mystery

It was a dark, rainy night when Mark and Lisa decided to go on their ghost hunt. They opened the back door slowly and quietly to make sure they didn't disturb their sleeping parents. Mark went first, tiptoeing down the gravel path. Lisa ran on the wet grass. As they closed the garden gate and entered the woodland, they were sure they heard faint whispers and muffled laughter. Surely not. Not at this hour...

Games for Building
Social Skills **BRIGHT IDEAS**

Gameboard

40 FINISH	39	38	37	36
31	32	33	34	35
30	29	28	27	26
21	22	23	24	25
20	19	18	17	16
11	12	13	14	15
10	9	8	7	6
1 START	2	3	4	5

Weather warning cards

Knights of old

● **Can you reach the castle to claim the treasure?**

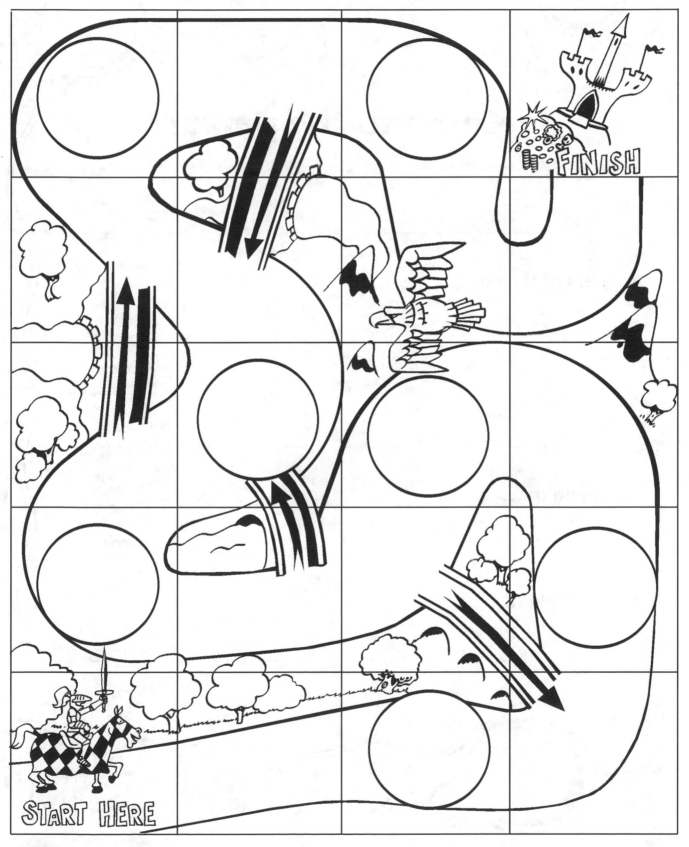

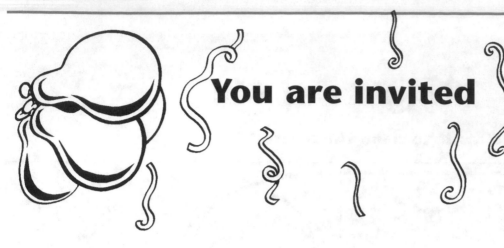

You are invited

Come to the party!

Name:

_____

Address of the party:

_____

_____

_____

Time and date:

_____

Please reply to:

_____

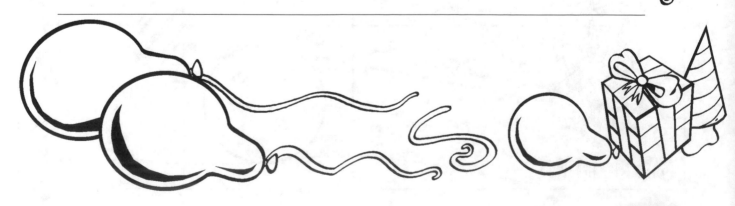

Games for Building
Social Skills

BRIGHT
IDEAS

CHAPTER 2

Co-operation and collaboration

AGE RANGE 7–11

LEARNING OBJECTIVE
To work as a member of a group to complete a given task.

CURRICULUM LINKS
QCA citizenship, Unit 1: Taking part.

Jigsaw

What you need
Scissors; A4 scrap paper (enough of each for one per child); thin A4 card; pencil crayons; felt-tipped pens; pencils (enough for one per group of two to four children); access to colour photocopiables, if possible.

What to do
● Put the class into groups of between two to four children. Give each group scissors and scrap paper, and invite each child to practise cutting up the paper into jigsaw-sized pieces. Explain that cutting very small pieces is difficult and cutting large pieces is too easy. Cutting about 20 pieces from each sheet of paper is ideal.

● Encourage the children to cut pieces with straight edges only for those pieces that would form the outside of a jigsaw.

● When the children are confident in cutting pieces of manageable proportions tell them you want them to create a jigsaw in their groups.

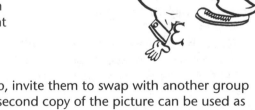

● Give each group a piece of thin card and drawing materials. Tell them to think of a picture as a group and nominate one child to draw the picture on the card. Suggest they draw the outline details with a pencil first and then colour in their picture. Each group member could colour a different part

● When their pictures are finished, make a colour copy on a photocopier so that each group has two versions of their picture.

● Then ask the children to draw around individual shapes or figures in their pictures in black. This will give clear definition to different shapes and the children can cut round them to make the jigsaw pieces. This is also helpful when the jigsaw is being put together.

● Once the groups have cut their pictures up, invite them to swap with another group and challenge them to make the jigsaw. The second copy of the picture can be used as a guide.

● After the activity is completed, encourage the children to share tips on how to create pictures more efficiently in their groups.

Differentiation
Let more able children use the same method to create more complicated jigsaw patterns. Ask less able children to time each other. Who can complete a jigsaw in the fastest time?

AGE RANGE 5–6

LEARNING OBJECTIVE
To work as one of a pair to complete a task; to use discussion to achieve a satisfactory outcome.

CURRICULUM LINKS
QCA citizenship, Unit 2: Choices.

Moving house

What you need
A selection of doll's house furniture; doll's house figures (enough for the children to have a selection of each, working in pairs); a model house or a doll's house.

What to do
● The object of the activity is to encourage the children to work together in pairs to furnish a house for a family.
● Put the class into pairs. Give each pair some doll's house furniture and figures.
● The first task for the children is to agree the composition of the family and give names to the family members. Remember to be sensitive to any children who have difficult family situations.
● Then invite the pairs, one at a time, to use the doll's house. Ask the children to name the rooms in the house and discuss how to layout the furniture in each room.
● Invite the children to furnish the rooms in the house, using the furniture they were given. They must discuss in their pairs how they will decide which furniture should go into each room. They also need to discuss where in the rooms the items should go.
● Tell the children that they must agree between them what their layout will look like. Suggest that they carry out this discussion as part of a role-play. They should each take on the role of a family member and express the opinions that they think the character is most likely to have. For example, Dad may want to have the TV in the living room, while his son may want it in his bedroom.

● Once the children have decided on their final layout and placed their furniture, they can discuss the layout with an adult. It is important to listen to and observe the discussion and negotiation that is taking place between the children.

Differentiation
Pair a less able child with a more able child, who can act as a supervisor. The supervisor can instruct their partner where to place the furniture. Offer pairs of more able children a given scenario that they have to consider before starting to move the furniture in. For example, the mother has been ill and cannot climb stairs, or the family have no money and cannot heat all of the rooms in the house.

AGE RANGE 7–11

LEARNING OBJECTIVE
To use a simple science experiment as a basis for co-operation, negotiation and discussion.

CURRICULUM LINKS
QCA citizenship, Unit 1: Taking part.

Jet aeroplanes

What you need
Non-inflated balloons (enough for the children to work in pairs); plastic drinking straws; sticky tape; scissors; a balloon pump; a large length of string (not wool); drawing pins; a board and writing materials.

What to do
● This fun activity offers opportunities for the children to compete against others in a race situation.
● Put the class into pairs. Give each pair a set of resources and explain to the children that the objective of the activity is to work together to create balloon jets. Then they will compete against other pairs to see who can get their balloon jet to travel the farthest along a line of string.
● Show the children how to create the jet balloon and string line.
● Cut a plastic straw in half and thread one half on to the string.
● Using the drawing pins, one at each end, stretch the string and pin it across the room. The string must be as taut as possible.
● Blow up a balloon. Do not tie the end, but hold it tightly when it is full of air.
● Using a small piece of sticky tape, and still holding the balloon so that the air does not escape, stick the balloon on to the straw. The balloon must be stuck on so that the hole is pointing in the same direction as the string, to allow the air to blow out of the back.
● Let go of the balloon. It should move along the piece of string like a jet aeroplane! Measure how far it travels along the string and record this on the board.
● Challenge a pair to come and race their jet balloon.
● Suggest that other pairs think of modifications to make their jet balloon travel further along the string.
● The pair whose jet balloon travels the farthest are the winners.

Differentiation
Let more able children write a manual for creating a top quality jet balloon. Encourage less able children to verbalise the process that they have followed. Check they are able to sequence the different steps they took to make a jet balloon.

AGE RANGE 5–11

LEARNING OBJECTIVE
To work with a partner to guide them through a simple course using only verbal instructions; to consider the consequences of our actions.

CURRICULUM LINKS
QCA citizenship, Unit 1: Taking part; Unit 4: People who help us.

Blindfold obstacle course

What you need

Two skipping ropes; a blindfold; small obstacles to use as stepping stones, such as small blocks or mats; access to the hall, playground or other large clear space; Health and Safety requirements must be carefully considered during the activity.

What to do

- Before the lesson begins, use the skipping ropes to create a simple two-sided path. Initially make the path very straight and defined.
  - At the beginning of the lesson, divide the class into pairs.
  - Show the children the rope path and explain that one child in each pair will be blindfolded. The other child will act as their guide and lead their blindfolded partner through the rope path using simple instructions, such as right, left, forwards, backwards and stop.
  - Some children may be nervous about using a blindfold, so let them close their eyes instead.
- Emphasise that guidance can only be given verbally and that the guide is not allowed to touch his or her partner.
- Tell the children that the object is to walk along the path without stepping over the skipping ropes, but that it is not a race.
- When one child in the pair has had a go, let them reverse the roles in their pair.
- Let other pairs take their turns. As the children become increasingly confident, small obstacles may be introduced to the path, such as a small block that they must step over.
- The children can also be encouraged to set up their own paths for each other, increasing the complexity of the path as they increase their skills.

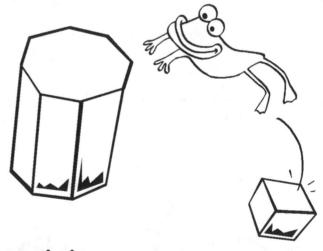

Differentiation

More able children may like to draw some obstacle course designs. They could then build these courses. At first, less able children may need to be paired with an adult so that instructions for walking along the path can be as clear as possible.

AGE RANGE 6–11

LEARNING OBJECTIVE
To guide a group to the treasure using codes; to listen and respond to information.

CURRICULUM LINKS
QCA citizenship, Unit 1: Taking part; Unit 8: How do rules and laws affect me?

Seek and find

What you need
Photocopiable page 33, one per child, and one per group of four children; counters; pencils.

What to do
● Give each child a copy of photocopiable page 33 and tell them that this is their treasure map.
● Practise using grid co-ordinates with the children. Read out a grid co-ordinate, such as B4, and ask the children to place a counter on the appropriate square on their map.
● Ask the children to draw various geographical features on their maps in a square or squares. Examples might include mountains covering B2, C2 and D2, or a river running through A1, A2, A3 and B4. Explain that these features must be kept secret.
● When the children have finished, tell them to decide secretly on which square of the map their treasure is hidden. Tell them that they are all now known as 'treasure guardians'.
● Put the children into groups of four and give them a blank copy of photocopiable page 33.
● Ask each group to elect one treasure guardian. Explain that the other members of the group must try to find the treasure guardian's treasure. Taking it in turns, they must give the treasure guardian a grid co-ordinate.
● The treasure guardian is only allowed to give very basic information:
1) The geographical feature, if there is one on the co-ordinate.
2) *Blank* if there is no feature at all.
3) *Treasure* if the child has discovered the co-ordinate where the treasure is hidden.

● Tell the groups that they should record the information the treasure guardian gives them on their blank treasure map. This will help them build up an idea of the treasure guardian's map and lead them to the treasure.
● The child who guesses the whereabouts of the treasure becomes the next treasure guardian and the game is repeated.

Differentiation
Let groups of more able children work together and encourage them to use compass directions to guide the group to the treasure. For example, if a child says *B5*, the treasure guardian can say *North*, if the treasure is hidden north of B5. Some children may find co-ordinates difficult to manage. Let these children work in pairs to interpret the information and also use co-ordinates more effectively.

AGE RANGE 9–11

LEARNING OBJECTIVE
To work as a group to assemble a structure using given resources.

CURRICULUM LINKS
QCA citizenship, Unit 1: Taking part; Unit 10 Local democracy for young citizens.

Top team

What you need
Construction resources, such as LEGO.

What to do
● Put the class into groups of four. Tell the groups that they are going to assemble a structure.
● Give each member of the group a specific role and explain that they must limit themselves to that role. The roles are Instructor, Supervisor and Drones.

● Explain that the Supervisor will tell the Instructor what must be done. The Instructor will tell the Drones what must be done and how to actually create the structure. The Drones will complete the actual building of the structure to the Instructor's specifications.
● Tell the groups that the structure should be of simple specification to begin with, and the Supervisor and Instructor must be very precise with their instructions.
● Gather all the Supervisors together and tell them what the structure that you want their group to build will be. For example, a wall.
● The Supervisors then go back to their groups and start the process. For example:
Supervisor: *Use 25 bricks and build a wall.*
Instructor: *Use 25 bricks and build a wall. Make the wall two bricks wide and five bricks high.*
● Encourage the groups to use terms such as: adjacent to and at an angle of 90 degrees.

Differentiation
With more able children, let the Supervisor draw the structure and offer this to the Instructor as a guide. For less able children, discuss the key features of the structure before they start. For example, discuss what will make the wall strong and what key facts should be considered when building the wall.

AGE RANGE 5–6

LEARNING OBJECTIVE
To create a 'road' for vehicles to use; to work co-operatively to overcome challenges.

CURRICULUM LINKS
QCA citizenship, Unit 1: Taking part; Unit 10: Local democracy for young citizens.

Drivers' delight

What you need
An example of a simple road map; a board and writing materials; thin A3 card; small cars and trucks; pencils; crayons and felt-tipped pens.

What to do
● Put the class into groups. Tell the children you want them to create their own road on A3 card. It needs to be big enough for small cars and trucks to travel along.
● Show the simple road map to the children and discuss the different features of roads, for example: roundabouts, crossroads, traffic lights and zebra crossings.
● Give the children simple instructions, and drawings to assist those who find reading challenging, relating to the content of the road. These might include: *Your road must have two crossroads, one roundabout and a cycle lane.* Write these on the board to remind the children as they create their roads.
● Give a sheet of A3 card, writing materials and the vehicles to each group. Remind them that their road needs to be wide enough to accommodate the cars and trucks.
● When the children have finished drawing the layout of their road, invite each group to talk to the rest of the class about it, highlighting what they are finding difficult and the ideas that they have incorporated.
● Allow the children time to use crayons and felt-tipped pens to decorate their road maps and to add any other ideas that they may have thought of during their discussion of all the layouts.
● When the groups have finished, place all their work together on the floor to create a huge road. This could be used in the playground and introduced to a wider audience at playtimes.

Differentiation
For more able children, increase the number of requirements for their roads and introduce safety features highlighting how children should cross the road safely. Limit the number of features for those children who will find the activity challenging. Gradually build the complexity as they grow in confidence and ability.

AGE RANGE 5–6

LEARNING OBJECTIVE
To sort resources into sets; to agree the way to sort resources as a group.

CURRICULUM LINKS
QCA citizenship, Unit 1: Taking part.

Sort it out!

What you need
A variety of resources to use for sorting into sets (consider using natural items you may have, such as stones or shells).

What to do
● Put the children into groups of four and give each group a selection of resources.
● Ask the groups to sort their items into sets. Give no guidance as to the type of sets required at this point.
● Tell them that you would like them to think about how the items can be grouped together and that you would like them to decide on the sets within their groups.
● Go around the groups while the children complete this task, and discuss the sets with the whole class when they have finished. Talk about how each group decided upon the criteria for the sets.
● Invite the children to re-sort the items into different sets. This time give them attributes to consider in their sorting, such as colour, size, shape and thickness.
● Encourage the children to co-operate with other group members as they do this. Invite them to share their ideas with each other and agree as to the criteria that is to be used to sort the sets.
● Increase the complexity of the task by providing more specific sorting instructions, such as sorting the logic blocks by size, colour and shape. This will make the task more challenging by increasing the number of attributes to consider.
● Let the groups repeat the activity using different resources.

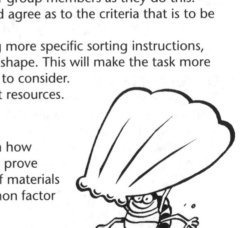

Differentiation
Invite more able children to provide instructions on how to sort the resources. Where the activity is going to prove challenging for children, provide them with a set of materials and ask them if they can identify what is the common factor with all the items in the set.

AGE RANGE 7–11

LEARNING OBJECTIVE
To work together, giving and following instructions in pairs; to complete a picture on a given theme.

CURRICULUM LINKS
QCA citizenship, Unit 1: Taking part.

Picture partners

What you need
A board and writing materials; A4 paper; pencils; coloured pencils, crayons and felt-tipped pens.

What to do
● Explain to the children that you want them to produce a picture on a given theme in their pairs. However, only one child from each pair will actually draw the picture. The other child will provide instructions to guide their partner with the drawing.
● Discuss with the children the most effective ways to instruct their partners and ask them to give examples. Write these on the board. Make sure the children include being precise in their requirements and instructing their partners in as much detail as possible, for example, by carefully describing the shapes and colours in each part of the picture.
● Give the children a simple theme for their pictures. This can be linked to a current topic or subject, a mood or a type of art. For example, graffiti, sad or happy, outer space, Henry VIII.
● Give each pair a piece of paper and drawing materials, and tell the children which of them will be the instructor and which the artist.
● Ask the instructors to begin by outlining which drawing materials and colours should be used.
● Explain to the children that it is easier if they instruct the artists to draw the outline of the picture in pencil first, as this is likely to require the greatest amount of instruction. They can then instruct their partner on how to fill in the outline.
● Let each pair discuss their completed pictures. Encourage them to talk about outline the most challenging parts of the activity and what they could have done better.
● Ask the pairs to then discuss their conclusions with the whole class.

Differentiation
For those children who have competent verbal skills, ask them to draw their own picture first, which is not seen by their partner. They should instruct their partner to draw the same picture and compare the two at the end. For children who find the activity challenging, give them specific features that they must include within their picture. For example, *I want you to draw a Roman soldier. He must have a shield, a helmet and a spear.*

AGE RANGE 6–11

LEARNING OBJECTIVE
To play a game against an opponent abiding by the rules, penalties and bonuses allowed.

CURRICULUM LINKS
QCA citizenship, Unit 8: How do rules and laws affect me?

Pest!

Fly

What you need
Two thin card copies of photocopiable page 34 for each pair of children; dice; coloured counters; pencils; coloured pencils; scissors.

What to do
● Put the class into pairs and explain that they are going to play a board game.
● Give each pair two card copies of photocopiable page 34. Explain that one will be used as the game board. They should cut the other up into the individual squares. They should be left with 33 blank squares; the Start and Finish squares can be discarded.
● Tell the children to draw a garden pest on 11 of their small squares, such as slugs, snails or greenfly. When they have completed these, tell them to place the ten 'pest' squares on different squares on the gameboard.
● Tell the children to write the word *Decoy* on another 11 cards. They should then place these one at a time on different squares on the gameboard.
● The final 11 cards can be used as 'forfeit' cards. Write ten categories on the board that the children should copy on to each of these cards. Examples might include, boys' names, girls' names, towns and cities, colours, rivers, seven times table, and so on. These are kept face down in a pile in front of the players.
● Explain the rules of the game to the children:
● When a player lands on a 'pest' square with their counter, they must pay a forfeit. They turn over the top forfeit card in the pile and throw the die. If, for example, a player picks up a forfeit card that says *Boys' names* and throws a six on the die, the player must give the names of six boys to pay the forfeit.
● If the questions are answered correctly, the player may proceed and have another go.
● If the questions are answered incorrectly, the player misses a go and proceeds on his or her next throw of the die.
● If a player lands on a 'decoy' card, they carry on as normal, waiting for their next turn.
● The winner is the player who gets through the vegetable patch first.

Slug

Snail

Differentiation
Allow more able children to modify the rules. Encourage them to include more penalties and bonuses, or to write out a new set of rules and invite a second pair to play the game. For those children who find the game challenging, limit the number of penalties, perhaps only having five 'pest' cards.

Seek and find

	A	B	C	D	E
1					
2					
3					
4					
5					
6					
7					

Pest!

31	32	33	34	35 FINISH
30•	29	28	27	26
21	22	23	24	25
20•	19	18	17	16
11	12	13	14	15
10•	9	8	7	6
1 START	2	3	4	5

CHAPTER 3

Moral values

AGE RANGE 5–11

LEARNING OBJECTIVE
To consider other people's feelings; to know how they can make a positive difference; to link action and consequences.

CURRICULUM LINKS
QCA citizenship, Unit 1: Taking part; Unit 2: Choices.

Can I play?

What you need
Photocopiable page 49 copied on to card, enough for one per child; split pins; copies of the dilemma, below, for each group; a board and writing materials.

What to do
● Give each child a Decision Wheel and show them how to pin the arrows on.
● Put the class into groups of four to six and tell the children they are now all Decision Makers.
● Read the dilemma, below, to the children and give each group a copy. Ask them to consider the dilemma in their heads and think about what they might do in this situation. Tell them to indicate their choice on their Decision Wheel by moving an arrow (they could indicate two options by using both arrows if they wish). Emphasise that there are no right and wrong answers.
● Ask the children to share their decisions with their group.
For example, *I'd go and play with someone else*; *I'd go into the corner and cry*; *I'd tell an adult*; *I'd remember this and try to get some other friends to do exactly the same to them another time.*
● Stop the groups after a short time and tell them you want them to consider the possible good and bad outcomes of some of the choices they have talked about.
● Go around the groups as they do this and encourage them to broaden the discussion to include individual children's feelings and how they might overcome these.
● Remind the groups that they are all Decision Makers and that you want them to reach a group decision about how they would respond to the dilemma. Explain that it is acceptable
not to reach a unanimous decision and, if so, they should go with the majority opinion.
● Record each group's solution on the board and discuss each with the whole class.

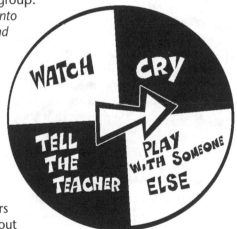

Dilemma
It's lunchtime and most of the children are in the playground playing. You go out to play. Some of your friends are playing and it looks like a good game. You ask if you can play too. They say *no*. How does this make you feel? What do you do next?

Differentiation
More able children could verbally discuss the processes they took to reach their decisions. Less able children could prepare a short drama based on the dilemma to use as a class (or whole school) assembly.

AGE RANGE 7–8

LEARNING OBJECTIVE
To consider stealing and if it is acceptable under any circumstances.

CURRICULUM LINKS
QCA citizenship, Unit 1: Taking part; Unit 2: Choices.

Mum's birthday treat

What you need
Photocopiable page 49 copied on to card, enough for one per child; split pins; copies of the dilemma, below, for each group; a board and writing materials.

What to do
● Give each child a Decision Wheel and show them how to pin the arrows on.
● Put the class into groups of four to six and tell the children they are now all Decision Makers.
● Read the dilemma, below, to the children and give each group a copy. Ask them to consider the dilemma in their heads and think about what they might do in this situation. Tell them to indicate their choice on their Decision Wheel by moving an arrow (they could indicate two options by using both arrows if they wish). Emphasise that there are no right and wrong answers.
● Ask the children to share their decisions with their group. For example, *Dan is only trying to be kind. It's a nice thought to get something for his mum; He's a mate, of course I'll do it; I might get caught; It's stealing.*
● Stop the groups after a short time and tell them you want them to consider the possible good and bad outcomes of some of the choices they have talked about.
● Go around the groups as they do this and encourage them to broaden the discussion to include individual children's feelings and how they might overcome these.
● Remind the groups that they are all Decision Makers and that you want them to reach a group decision about how they would respond to the dilemma. Explain that it is acceptable not to reach a unanimous decision and, if so, they should go with the majority.
● Record each group's solution on the board and discuss each with the whole class.

> **Dilemma**
> Riding on your bike, you meet two friends, Dan and Ryan. Dan explains that it's his mum's birthday. He has no money to buy her a present, so he asks you to 'cover' for him at the local sweetshop while he takes a box of chocolates without paying.

Differentiation
More able children may discuss the implications of stealing in a range of situations: from home, a shop, or a friend's house. Less able children can be encouraged to draw pictures or write the names of the emotions that each person is likely to be feeling in the dilemma.

Games for Building
Social Skills

We don't want you!

AGE RANGE 5–11

LEARNING OBJECTIVE
To understand that isolation from friends can be unpleasant; to consider appropriate responses in such situations.

CURRICULUM LINKS
QCA citizenship, Unit 1: Taking part; Unit 2: Choices.

What you need
Photocopiable page 49 copied on to card, enough for one per child; split pins; copies of the dilemma, below, for each group; a board and writing materials.

What to do
● Give each child a Decision Wheel and show them how to pin the arrows on.
● Put the class into groups of four to six and tell the children they are now all Decision Makers.
● Read the dilemma, below, to the children and give each group a copy. Ask them to consider the dilemma in their heads and think about what they might do in this situation. Tell them to indicate their choice on their Decision Wheel by moving an arrow (they could indicate two options by using both arrows if they wish). Emphasise that there are no right and wrong answers.
● Ask the children to share their decisions with their group. For example, *I'd ignore Salma and play with my other friends; I'd get others to be horrible to Salma; I'd pull faces at Salma and make rude remarks about her.*
● Stop the groups after a short time and tell them you want them to consider the possible good and bad outcomes of some of the choices they have talked about.
● Go around the groups as they do this and encourage them to broaden the discussion to include individual children's feelings and how they might overcome these.
● Remind the groups that they are all Decision Makers and that you want them to reach a group decision about how they would respond to the dilemma. Explain that they should go with the majority opinion.
● Record each group's solution on the board and discuss each with the whole class.

> ### Dilemma
> It's lunchtime. You and your friends are out in the playground. You decide you want to play a particular game. Your friend Salma says she wants to play something else. You won't. She tells the rest of the group to ignore you and play with her. They do. You're cross with Salma – very cross. Salma's left you out and you're on your own. Now what?

Differentiation
More able children can use the dilemma as a basis to create a drama. Less able children could create posters to use in the playground to remind the children how to care for and respect each other.

AGE RANGE 5–11

LEARNING OBJECTIVE
To know that telling on other children is often considered taboo, to consider whether it should be and what they can do about this.

CURRICULUM LINKS
QCA citizenship, Unit 1: Taking part; Unit 2: Choices.

Cry baby!

What you need
Photocopiable page 49 copied on to card, enough for one per child; split pins; copies of the dilemma, below, for each group; a board and writing materials.

What to do
● Give each child a Decision Wheel and show them how to pin the arrows on.
● Put the class into groups of four to six and tell the children they are now all Decision Makers.
● Read the dilemma, below, to the children and give each group a copy. Ask them to consider the dilemma in their heads and think about what they might do in this situation. Tell them to indicate their choice on their Decision Wheel by moving an arrow (they could indicate two options by using both arrows if they wish). Emphasise that there are no right and wrong answers.
● Ask the children to share their decisions with their group. For example, *I'd ask Fred who these boys are and go and sort them out; I'd get some friends together and get them to help me sort these boys out; I'd stay and look after Fred; I'd go and tell a lunchtime supervisor.*
● Stop the groups after a short time and tell them you want them to consider the possible good and bad outcomes of some of the choices they have talked about.
● Go around the groups as they do this and encourage them to broaden the discussion to include individual children's feelings and how they might overcome these.
● Remind the groups that they are all Decision Makers and that you want them to reach a group decision about how they would respond to the dilemma.
● Record each group's solution on the board and discuss each with the whole class.

> **Dilemma**
> You and Fred are the best of friends. He looks after you and you look after him. One lunchtime you find him near to tears (in fact he's trying hard not to cry). He tells you that some of the other boys have been horrible – really horrible. He's scared and he's upset. What do you do?

Differentiation
Less able children could invite a lunchtime supervisor to come and discuss some of the issues they have to manage with the class. More able children can write newspaper articles with eye-catching headlines on this theme.

AGE RANGE 6–11

LEARNING OBJECTIVE
To examine and verbalise what anger feels like; to understand how to manage anger.

CURRICULUM LINKS
QCA citizenship, Unit 1: Taking part; Unit 2: Choices.

Ow! That hurts...

What you need
Photocopiable page 49 copied on to card, enough for one per child; split pins; copies of the dilemma, below, for each group; a board and writing materials.

What to do
● Give each child a Decision Wheel and show them how to pin the arrows on.
● Put the class into groups of four to six and tell the children they are now all Decision Makers.
● Read the dilemma, below, to the children and give each group a copy. Ask them to consider the dilemma in their heads and think about what they might do in this situation. Tell them to indicate their choice on their Decision Wheel by moving an arrow (they could indicate two options by using both arrows if they wish). Emphasise that there are no right and wrong answers. Each choice will have its own consequences.
● Ask the children to share their decisions with their group. For example, *I'd forget it; I'd get my own back even though I know I'll get into trouble.* Encourage the children to consider as wide a variety of solutions for this situation as possible.
● Stop the groups after a short time and tell them you want them to consider the possible good and bad outcomes of some of the choices they have talked about.
● Go around the groups as they do this and encourage them to broaden the discussion to include individual children's feelings and how they might overcome these.
● Remind the groups that they are all Decision Makers and that you want them to reach a group decision about how they would respond to the dilemma. Explain that it is acceptable not to reach a unanimous decision and, if so, they should go with the majority.
● Record each group's solution on the board and discuss each with the whole class.

> **Dilemma**
> You're out playing at school when you see Jonah. He was out playing yesterday. For no reason at all he kicked you hard. You remember this. It makes you mad... What do you do?

Differentiation
Less able children could role-play the dilemma. How would they cope in this situation? More able children can consider extension strategies to use in the playground. For example, supporting children when they are in trouble, upset or hurt. They could plan how to use these strategies and, with the help of others, introduce them.

AGE RANGE 7–11

LEARNING OBJECTIVE
To learn how to react to an adult's request when they think it is not fair.

CURRICULUM LINKS
QCA citizenship, Unit 1: Taking part; Unit 2: Choices.

Bossy boots

What you need
Photocopiable page 49 copied on to card, enough for one per child; split pins; copies of the dilemma, below, for each group; a board and writing materials.

What to do
● Give each child a Decision Wheel and show them how to pin the arrows on.
● Put the class into groups of four to six and tell the children they are now all Decision Makers.
● Read the dilemma, below, to the children and give each group a copy. Ask them to consider the dilemma in their heads and think about what they might do in this situation. Tell them to indicate their choice on their Decision Wheel by moving an arrow (they could indicate two options by using both arrows if they wish). Emphasise that there are no right and wrong answers.
● Ask the children to share their decisions with their group. For example, *She's not my teacher. I'd ignore what she said and stay where I am; I'd tell her I wasn't going to move anywhere.*
● Stop the groups after a short time and tell them you want them to consider the possible good and bad outcomes of some of the choices they have talked about.
● Go around the groups as they do this and encourage them to broaden the discussion to include individual children's feelings and how they might overcome these.
● Remind the groups that they are all Decision Makers and that you want them to reach a group decision about how they would respond to the dilemma. Explain that it is acceptable not to reach a unanimous decision and, if so, they should go with the majority.
● Record each group's solution on the board and discuss each with the whole class.

> **Dilemma**
> You and your friends are out to play at lunchtime. A lunchtime supervisor tells you to move away from the door. This is the last straw – she's not your teacher – it's the sixth time she's moaned at you. She can't tell you what to do. You've had enough! What do you do?

Differentiation
More able children can use this dilemma as a basis to widen a group or class discussion. How can children challenge adults when it is clear they are being unfair? Less able children can consider the theme of 'fair and unfair' using personal experiences and join in the more able children's discussions.

AGE RANGE 6–11

LEARNING OBJECTIVE
To consider if friends should be supported even when they are in the wrong.

CURRICULUM LINKS
QCA citizenship, Unit 1: Taking part; Unit 2: Choices.

He's my friend

What you need
Photocopiable page 49 copied on to card, enough for one per child; split pins; copies of the dilemma, below, for each group; a board and writing materials.

What to do
● Give each child a Decision Wheel and show them how to pin the arrows on.
● Put the class into groups of four to six and tell the children they are now all Decision Makers.
● Read the dilemma, below, to the children and give each group a copy. Ask them to consider the dilemma in their heads and think about what they might do in this situation. Tell them to indicate their choice on their Decision Wheel by moving an arrow (they could indicate two options by using both arrows if they wish). Emphasise that there are no right and wrong answers.
● Ask the children to share their decisions with their group. For example, *I'd refuse to speak to either Hassan or Joshua as they're both wrong; I'd stick with my good friend and ignore Joshua even though I know Hassan is wrong; I'd find an adult and tell them what happened.*
● Stop the groups after a short time and tell them you want them to consider the possible good and bad outcomes of some of the choices they have talked about.
● Go around the groups as they do this and encourage them to broaden the discussion to include individual children's feelings and how they might overcome these.
● Remind the groups that they are all Decision Makers and that you want them to reach a group decision about how they would respond to the dilemma. Explain that it is acceptable not to reach a unanimous decision and, if so, they should go with the majority.
● Record each group's solution on the board and discuss each with the whole class.

> ### Dilemma
> You come out into the playground. You've been told that Hassan kicked Joshua and that they had a fight. Hassan is a good friend. You don't like Joshua much. Hassan says that Joshua hit him with the football and threatened him. Joshua says that Hassan got in the way of the football game. Hassan says he kicked Joshua because he deserved it…

Differentiation
More able children can discuss what makes a good friend. Less able children can draw their ideal friend and write key friendship words around the edge of the picture.

AGE RANGE 5–11

LEARNING OBJECTIVE
To consider how far to go to protect a friend.

CURRICULUM LINKS
QCA citizenship, Unit 1: Taking part; Unit 2: Choices;
Unit 8: How do rules and laws affect me?

Keep the secret

What you need
Photocopiable page 49 copied on to card, enough for one per child; split pins; copies of the dilemma, below, for each group; a board and writing materials.

What to do
● Give each child a Decision Wheel and show them how to pin the arrows on.
● Put the class into groups of four to six and tell the children they are now all Decision Makers.
● Read the dilemma, below, to the children and give each group a copy. Ask them to consider the dilemma in their heads and think about what they might do in this situation. Tell them to indicate their choice on their Decision Wheel by moving an arrow (they could indicate two options by using both arrows if they wish). Emphasise that there are no right and wrong answers.
● Ask the children to share their decisions with their group. For example, *I would definitely go and tell on Amy; I'd pretend I hadn't seen anything and leave.*
● Stop the groups after a short time and tell them you want them to consider the possible good and bad outcomes of some of the choices they have talked about.
● Go around the groups as they do this and encourage them to broaden the discussion to include individual children's feelings and how they might overcome these.
● Remind the groups that they are all Decision Makers and that you want them to reach a group decision about how they would respond to the dilemma. Explain that it is acceptable not to reach a unanimous decision and, if so, they should go with the majority.
● Record each group's solution on the board and discuss each with the whole class.

> ### Dilemma
> There's been some trouble at school. In assembly Mrs Langdon mentioned that someone is damaging the toilets. The next day, you walk into the toilets and find your friend Amy. There's water everywhere and it's clear to you that she is the one who's been causing the problems. What do you do?

Differentiation
More able children can use this dilemma as the focus for work around the concept of rules. Why is it necessary to have group rules? What might occur without them? Less able children can look at the school rules, or rules for the playground or at lunchtime.

AGE RANGE 6–11

LEARNING OBJECTIVE
To consider how unfairness makes them feel and to think about what they can do about it.

CURRICULUM LINKS
QCA citizenship, Unit 1: Taking part; Unit 2: Choices.

It wasn't me

What you need
Photocopiable page 49 copied on to card, enough for one per child; split pins; copies of the dilemma, below, for each group; a board and writing materials.

What to do
- Give each child a Decision Wheel and show them how to pin the arrows on.
- Put the class into groups of four to six and tell the children they are now all Decision Makers.
- Read the dilemma, below, to the children and give each group a copy. Ask them to consider the dilemma in their heads and think about what they might do in this situation. Tell them to indicate their choice on their Decision Wheel by moving an arrow (they could indicate two options by using both arrows if they wish). Emphasise that there are no right and wrong answers.
- Ask the children to share their decisions with their group. For example, *I'd lose my temper; I'd get told off – I'm not bothered about the adult, but I'd want to make sure my friend believed it wasn't me; I'd just keep quiet and wait to get her later.*

- Stop the groups after a short time and tell them you want them to consider the possible good and bad outcomes of some of the choices they have talked about.
- Go around the groups as they do this and encourage them to broaden the discussion to include individual children's feelings and how they might overcome these.
- Remind the groups that they are all Decision Makers and that you want them to reach a group decision about how they would respond to the dilemma. Explain that they should go with the majority opinion.
- Record each group's solution on the board and discuss each with the whole class.

> **Dilemma**
> You're in the dining area ready to eat your lunch. Ellie, the class's naughty girl, is next to you and you can't move away from her. She starts throwing food about when the adults aren't watching. Some food hits your friend, who thinks you are to blame. Then one of the adults also thinks it's you. Ellie just laughs quietly while you get into trouble. What do you do?

Differentiation
More able children can use the dilemma as the basis for a drama. Less able children can create priority lists about being 'naughty'. What is really very naughty and what is mildly naughty?

AGE RANGE 5–11

LEARNING OBJECTIVE
To understand that bullying is wrong.

CURRICULUM LINKS
QCA citizenship, Unit 1: Taking part; Unit 2: Choices.

Bully for you

What you need
Photocopiable page 49 copied on to card, enough for one per child; split pins; copies of the dilemma, below, for each group; a board and writing materials.

What to do
● Give each child a Decision Wheel and show them how to pin the arrows on.
● Put the class into groups of four to six and tell the children they are now all Decision Makers.
● Read the dilemma, below, to the children and give each group a copy. Ask them to consider the dilemma in their heads and think about what they might do in this situation. Tell them to indicate their choice on their Decision Wheel by moving an arrow (they could indicate two options by using both arrows if they wish). Emphasise that there are no right and wrong answers.
● Ask the children to share their decisions with their group. For example, *I'd tell. It's wrong to bully; The teacher will ask us and I might say something then; I'd just keep quiet. It's none of my business.*
● Stop the groups after a short time and tell them you want them to consider the possible good and bad outcomes of some of the choices they have talked about.
● Go around the groups as they do this and encourage them to broaden the discussion to include individual children's feelings and how they might overcome these.
● Remind the groups that they are all Decision Makers and that you want them to reach a group decision about how they would respond to the dilemma.
● Record each group's solution on the board and discuss each with the whole class.

Dilemma
Some parents have complained that their children are being bullied at school. Some parents have said their children have been called names. Others have said that their children have been hit and kicked for no reason. No child is prepared to say who is doing this because they're so scared. You overhear some adults talking about this in the playground. You are in the bully's class and know who it is. What do you do?

Differentiation
More able children can use the dilemma as a focus for work on bullying. Ask them to investigate ideas to support the anti-bullying culture in the school. Less able children can create a display to remind children of the school's anti-bullying culture.

AGE RANGE 7–11

LEARNING OBJECTIVE
To learn to say 'no' to friends when asked to do something they do not want to.

CURRICULUM LINKS
QCA citizenship, Unit 1: Taking part; Unit 2: Choices.

Help your friend

What you need
Photocopiable page 49 copied on to card, enough for one per child; split pins; copies of the dilemma, below, for each group; a board and writing materials.

What to do
● Give each child a Decision Wheel and show them how to pin the arrows on.
● Put the class into groups of four to six and tell the children they are now all Decision Makers.
● Read the dilemma, below, to the children and give each group a copy. Ask them to consider the dilemma in their heads and think about what they might do in this situation. Tell them to indicate their choice on their Decision Wheel by moving an arrow (they could indicate two options by using both arrows if they wish). Emphasise that there are no right and wrong answers.

● Ask the children to share their decisions with their group. For example, *I don't agree with bullying, but David is a good friend so I'd probably join in (but I wouldn't hurt William – just scare him a bit); I'd try to stick up for William; I'd definitely say no.*
● Stop the groups after a short time and tell them you want them to consider the possible good and bad outcomes of some of the choices they have talked about.
● Go around the groups as they do this and encourage them to broaden the discussion to include individual children's feelings and how they might overcome these.
● Remind the groups that they are all Decision Makers and that you want them to reach a group decision about how they would respond to the dilemma. Explain that they should go with the majority opinion.
● Record each group's solution on the board and discuss each with the whole class.

Dilemma
David, one of your best friends, has been frightening another boy, William. William is really, really scared and manages to avoid coming into the playground most of the time. David wants you to get involved – perhaps outside school, because it's hard to get at William in school now. He says it will be a laugh to wait for William when he's on the way home and follow him. Then, just before he gets home, to take his bag and run off. What do you think?

Differentiation
More able children can use the dilemma as a focus for work on bullying. Less able children can create posters to reinforce the school's anti-bullying culture.

AGE RANGE 5–11

LEARNING OBJECTIVE
To consider what to do when they are blamed for something that is not their fault.

CURRICULUM LINKS
QCA citizenship, Unit 1: Taking part; Unit 2: Choices.

Not you again!

What you need
Photocopiable page 49 copied on to card, enough for one per child; split pins; copies of the dilemma, below, for each group; a board and writing materials.

What to do
● Give each child a Decision Wheel and show them how to pin the arrows on.
● Put the class into groups of four to six and tell the children they are now all Decision Makers.

● Read the dilemma, below, to the children and give each group a copy. Ask them to consider the dilemma in their heads and think about what they might do in this situation. Tell them to indicate their choice on their Decision Wheel by moving an arrow (they could indicate two options by using both arrows if they wish). Emphasise that there are no right and wrong answers.
● Ask the children to share their decisions with their group. For example, *The person who did it is a friend. I don't tell on my friends; I'd try to get the person who did it to own up; I'd tell the headteacher who it was and if they won't believe me my parents will.*
● Stop the groups after a short time and tell them you want them to consider the possible good and bad outcomes of some of the choices they have talked about.
● Go around the groups as they do this and encourage them to broaden the discussion to include individual children's feelings and how they might overcome these.
● Remind the groups that they are all Decision Makers and that you want them to reach a group decision about how they would respond to the dilemma. Explain that they should go with the majority opinion.
● Record each group's solution on the board and discuss each with the whole class.

> **Dilemma**
> You're in the classroom working. Everyone's a bit noisy, but that's not unusual. Someone shouts out swear words. The teacher, Mrs Prashad, thinks it's you. She is very annoyed and says she is going to tell your parents, you've got a week's detention and you're to go to the headteacher's room. It wasn't you who shouted out the swear words, but you know who it was and she's a good friend. What do you do?

Differentiation
Let less able children role-play the dilemma. Ask more able children to discuss reasonable punishments for different levels of 'naughtiness' in the classroom.

AGE RANGE 5–11

LEARNING OBJECTIVE
To understand the difficulties when they do not like someone and the problems it causes; to understand that they should behave respectfully in a difficult situation.

CURRICULUM LINKS
QCA citizenship, Unit 1: Taking part; Unit 2: Choices.

Go away!

What you need
Photocopiable page 49 copied on to card, enough for one per child; split pins; copies of the dilemma, below, for each group; a board and writing materials.

What to do
● Give each child a Decision Wheel and show them how to pin the arrows on.
● Put the class into groups of four to six and tell the children they are now all Decision Makers.
● Read the dilemma, below, to the children and give each group a copy. Ask them to consider the dilemma in their heads and think about what they might do in this situation. Tell them to indicate their choice on their Decision Wheel by moving an arrow (they could indicate two options by using both arrows if they wish). Emphasise that there are no right and wrong answers.
● Ask the children to share their decisions with their group. For example, *I'd go and tell an adult and get him or her to get rid of Emma; I'd tell Emma again to push off.*
● Stop the groups after a short time and tell them you want them to consider the possible good and bad outcomes of some of the choices they have talked about.
● Go around the groups as they do this and encourage them to broaden the discussion to include individual children's feelings and how they might overcome these.
● Remind the groups that they are all Decision Makers and that you want them to reach a group decision about how they would respond to the dilemma. Explain that they should go with the majority opinion.
● Record each group's solution on the board and discuss each with the whole class.

Dilemma
Emma is always trying to push into your group of friends. She's a pain really. You've told her she's not welcome, but she keeps coming back. One of the reasons you don't like Emma is that she can be really babyish. If she gets in a temper, she screams and cries like a two-year-old. On this day, you've told her to push off again. At lunchtime, she still tries to join in. What do you do?

Differentiation
Let less able children draw friendship trees. Ask them who their best friends are and why. More able children can consider their own personalities. What do they consider are their strengths. What areas for improvement are there?

AGE RANGE 5–11

LEARNING OBJECTIVE
To consider how to react when someone hurts them.

CURRICULUM LINKS
QCA citizenship, Unit 1: Taking part; Unit 2: Choices.

Horrible mates

What you need
Photocopiable page 49 copied on to card, enough for one per child; split pins; copies of the dilemma, below, for each group; a board and writing materials.

What to do
● Give each child a Decision Wheel and show them how to pin the arrows on.
● Put the class into groups of four to six and tell the children they are now all Decision Makers.
● Read the dilemma, below, to the children and give each group a copy. Ask them to consider the dilemma in their heads and think about what they might do in this situation. Tell them to indicate their choice on their Decision Wheel by moving an arrow (they could indicate two options by using both arrows if they wish). Emphasise that there are no right and wrong answers.
● Ask the children to share their decisions with their group. For example, *I'd get some of my friends to sort Rachel out; I'd join the game and then get my own back; I'd burst into tears and run and tell an adult.*
● Stop the groups after a short time and tell them you want them to consider the possible good and bad outcomes of some of the choices they have talked about.
● Go around the groups as they do this and encourage them to broaden the discussion to include individual children's feelings and how they might overcome these.
● Remind the groups that they are all Decision Makers and that you want them to reach a group decision about how they would respond to the dilemma. Explain that they should go with the majority opinion.
● Record each group's solution on the board and discuss each with the whole class.

Dilemma
You are playing quietly with a group of friends when a ball hits you. It hurts more than usual because a stone has got caught up in it. Rachel, who is involved in the ball game, runs up and pushes you.
  'You idiot,' she says. 'Keep out of the way or I'll knock your head off.'
You know this Rachel and you don't like her. She's selfish and nasty. You are mad (really mad!). What do you do?

Differentiation
Less able children can draw pictures of common difficulties the children face in the playground. Agree as a class how these can be overcome. More able children can create a display of these pictures, with captions, to share with other children.

The Decision Wheel

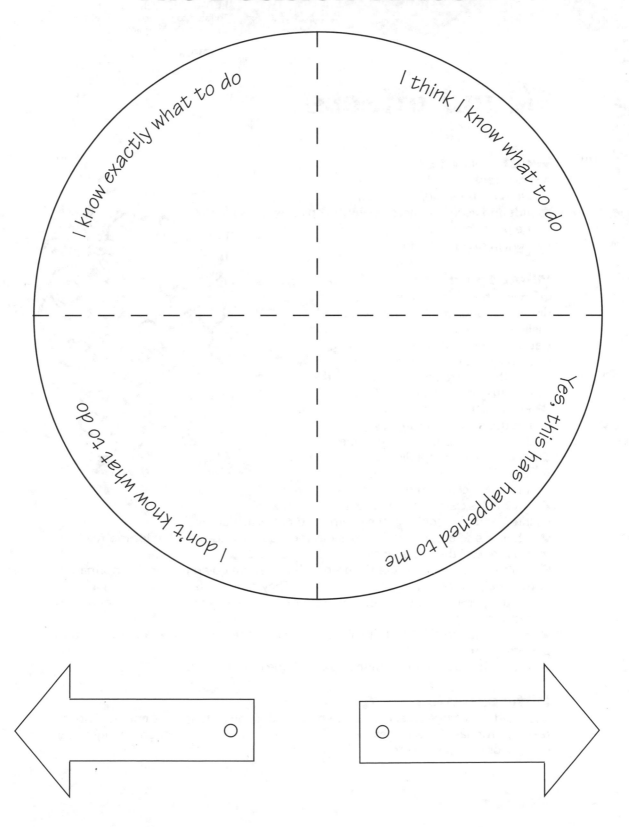

CHAPTER 4

Listening and speaking

AGE RANGE 5–11

LEARNING OBJECTIVE
To listen to a simple story, and use actions and sounds to accompany it.

CURRICULUM LINKS
QCA citizenship, Unit 1: Taking part.

Sound effects

What you need

A short story or poem that will act as a medium for the children to introduce body sounds and actions to accompany it; copies of the poem or story, enough for the children to work in groups of four.

What to do

● Invite the children to experiment and discover sounds they can make using their voice, hands and body. For example, clapping their hands, tapping their feet, singing a note or humming.
● Ask the children to share some of the sounds they made with the class.
● Read the poem or story to the children, asking them to listen carefully.
● Ask them to listen a second time to allow them to retain the storyline or poem content.
● Talk about the different sounds and actions that occur in the story or poem.
● Divide the class into groups of four children and give copies of the poem or story to each group.
● Choose one group member to act as the reader (or use an adult for this role). Tell the readers to read the poem or story to their groups.
● Tell the other members of the groups that they are going to give a performance of the poem or story as it is being read out. They cannot use dialogue, but have to accompany the text with actions and sounds using their voice, hands and bodies (but no instruments).
● Encourage the children to think about what happens in the text and to take turns in performing sounds and actions.
● Ask each group to perform their piece to the rest of the class.

Differentiation

Allow older, or more able, children to prepare their own stories and poems. Choose texts appropriate for each year group. Allow older children to support younger year groups, or less able children.

AGE RANGE 5–11

LEARNING OBJECTIVE
To distinguish between different sounds, and identify untuned musical instruments by listening.

CURRICULUM LINKS
QCA citizenship, Unit 1: Taking part.

Shake it!

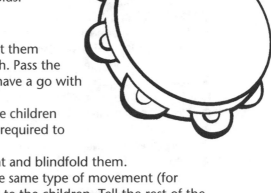

What you need
A wide variety of untuned instruments that can be shaken or scraped, such as bells, maracas, tambourines; blindfolds.

What to do
● Show the children the musical instruments and let them hear the different sounds that can be made with each. Pass the instruments around the class so that each child can have a go with each instrument.
● Name the instruments carefully and make sure the children know what each instrument is called, as they will be required to name them in the activity.
● Ask for one or two volunteers to come to the front and blindfold them.
● Initially, begin with two instruments and using the same type of movement (for example, scraping or shaking) play both instruments to the children. Tell the rest of the class to watch silently.
● Ask the children who are blindfolded to guess which instruments they can hear. Can they name them? Can they guess the movement that is being applied to each instrument?
● Let other children come and be blindfolded, and guess the instruments in the same way.
● After each child has had a go, encourage the class to talk about whether it was difficult or easy to guess the instrument and movement. Encourage them to talk about the different ways you can make sounds with the instruments.
● As the children become more skilled in listening and distinguishing between the different sounds, increase the number of instruments they have to guess. This will encourage them to really listen carefully and to listen for longer periods.

Differentiation
Let more able children take a more active role, playing the instruments to those who are blindfolded. For less able children, use pictures of the instruments. With their backs turned to the players, they can point to the correct picture when it is played.

AGE RANGE 4–11

LEARNING OBJECTIVE
To learn a song and substitute sounds for some of the words.

CURRICULUM LINKS
QCA citizenship, Unit 1: Taking part. QCA music, Unit 1: Ongoing skills.

Story song

What you need
A simple cumulative song, such as 'I Went to the Animal Fair' or 'This Old Man'.

What to do
● Tell the children that they are going to sing a cumulative song such as 'This Old Man' and as it progresses they are going to leave out a word and substitute it with an action. The challenge will be how many words they can leave out!
● Teach the children the song. They will need to know it very well. A good way of helping them to start with is as follows:
● Sing the first line. Ask the children to repeat it.
● Sing the second line. Ask the children to repeat it.
● Sing the third line, and so on.
● When you reach the end of the song, begin again. This time, sing the first and second lines to the children. Let them repeat these. Continue in this way, taking two lines at a time until the end of the song.
● Ask the children to sing the song all the way through with you. Then repeat the whole song two or three times until the children can sing it through with ease.
● Tell the children you want them to leave out a given word. Then repeat the song together, substituting an action for the missing word. This might be:

This old man, he played —— (use an action here to replace the missing word – one)
He played knick knack on my drum...

● Continue to sing the song together in this way, leaving out key words and substituting them with actions. How many words can the class confidently omit?
● Encourage the children to think of actions that they can use to substitute the words.
● When the children know the song really well, they can perform it in groups and decide themselves which words to omit and which actions to use.

Differentiation
More able children could teach other children a new song, or allow them to take the lead role and choose the words to be omitted. Less able children will need practice and support to remember to omit words and substitute actions. It may be helpful to display the words using an overhead projector or to write them on the board. Adults may like to warn them the word is about to be omitted, or use an aid to help them.

AGE RANGE 5–6

LEARNING OBJECTIVE
To recognise classmates' voices when blindfolded.

CURRICULUM LINKS
QCA citizenship, Unit 1: Taking part.

Blind man's bluff

What you need
A quiet area; a chair; a blindfold.

What to do
● Ask the class to stand in a circle.
● Ask for a volunteer to sit on a chair in the middle of the circle.
● Blindfold the volunteer and make sure that the child cannot see the other children in the circle. If any of the children are nervous of being blindfolded then they could put their hands over their eyes instead.
● Once the child in the middle has been blindfolded, ask the children in the circle to change places as silently as possible, so that the volunteer now has no idea of where anyone in the circle is standing.
● Once the children in the circle have settled in their new places, ask the volunteer to point at random at the circle. The volunteer should say, *Tell me, tell me, who are you?*
● The chosen child should reply in their normal speaking voice, *I can see you. Guess who I am.*
● The volunteer can then take one guess.
● If the volunteer is correct, the children can respond with a clap. If the volunteer is incorrect the children can give a groan!
● If an incorrect guess is given, the volunteer must have another go at pointing and guessing.
● When a correct guess is given, the chosen child can take the position in the chair, put on the blindfold and the game can begin again.

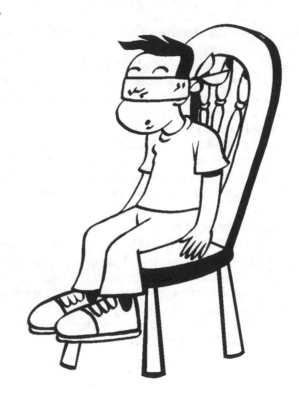

Differentiation
As children become increasingly competent they may disguise their voices if they are chosen to speak. When the group becomes well motivated and skilled, then try with two children speaking at once. Can the volunteer guess both children's names? If some children find the activity challenging, choose those who have distinctive voices and limit the number of children in the circle.

AGE RANGE 5–11

LEARNING OBJECTIVE
To manage silence appropriately; to listen quietly and concentrate for a given period of time.

CURRICULUM LINKS
QCA citizenship, Unit 1: Taking part.

Silence is golden

What you need
Candle and matches or a lava lamp; relaxing music, such as sea sounds or classical music.

What to do
● Some children find silence intimidating, as it can be alien to their world. This activity aims to encourage the children to respond positively to silence and to introduce the basic skills involved in relaxation.

● Start by using a visual stimulus, such as a lit candle or a slow-moving lava lamp. This will create the right atmosphere.

● Place the visual stimulus in front of the children and ask them to focus on the light or movement.

● Teach the children to concentrate while keeping eye contact with the lamp or candle. Encourage them to sit still and concentrate on their breathing. Help them by repeating, *in and out, in and out,* for them to breathe in time.

● When the group manages this consistently – and some will find it hard – introduce the group to quiet music to reinforce the atmosphere. Make sure they keep focusing on the visual stimulus too.

● When the children are happy with this, remove the visual stimulus and allow them to maintain their silence while listening to the music.

● Use the relaxation ideas as a regular feature of classroom life. With experience and regular use, it is possible to encourage children who are noisy or excitable (after running around at lunchtime, for example) to a calmer and more receptive state.

Differentiation
For children who find this activity particularly challenging, provide some steps to introduce them to the concept of silence. This might include watching a short cartoon or piece on television with the sound turned off. It is amazing how long some children will sit absolutely still while watching silent cartoons! For those children who are able to manage silence and engage positively with the basics of relaxation techniques, introduce them to creating a calm silent atmosphere without the use of music or visual stimulus. Can they create this using their skill?

Games for Building Social Skills

BRIGHT IDEAS

AGE RANGE 7–11

LEARNING OBJECTIVE
To encourage children to recognise a variety of emotions.

CURRICULUM LINKS
QCA citizenship, Unit 1: Taking part; Unit 2: Choices.

Are you cross?

What you need
Photocopiable page 62 copied on to card and cut up to form 'Emotion cards'; photocopiable page 63 copied on to card and cut up, enough for one set per child.

What to do
● Sit the children in a line facing the same way.
● Ask for a volunteer to come to the front and face the line of children. Let them choose an emotion card.
● Ask the volunteer to act in the way that the emotion card tells them. For example, if the card says *frightened*, then the child should act as though they are frightened.
● Encourage the volunteer to use speech and actions to convey the emotion.
● The rest of the class should try and guess which emotion the volunteer is displaying. Whoever guesses correctly is the next person to choose an emotion card and act out the emotion.
● After a while, bring the class back together and discuss how it is important to know how to tell what a person is feeling.
● Discuss the importance of recognising how friends are feeling. Ask the children to suggest how they can tell what mood their friends are in. Make sure they consider looking at their faces, looking at their body language and listening to what they are saying.
● Discuss appropriate responses to given situations. For example, how should they respond when someone is showing their anger?
● Give each child a set of pictures from photocopiable page 61 to emphasise how facial expressions can reveal emotions. Take each card in turn and ask the children to tell you how the people are feeling.

Differentiation
For less able children, use regular drama sessions to reinforce appropriate responses to others. Focus on the negative emotions that we all feel sometimes and keep the scenarios superficial, dealing with common problems the children may face. These might include, *I'm in a temper*. Allow the children to act out scenarios and practise giving suitable responses. More able children may use drama and focus on more complex issues, such as managing appropriate responses by being assertive, not aggressive.

AGE RANGE 7–11

LEARNING OBJECTIVE
To listen to and recognise common sounds that have been tape-recorded.

CURRICULUM LINKS
QCA citizenship, Unit 1: Taking part.

Guess the sound

What you need

Portable tape recorders (with counters on them); blank tapes; clipboards; photocopiable page 64; pencils; A4 paper (enough of each resource for the children to work in groups of four).

What to do

● Divide the children into groups of four.
● Give each group a tape recorder, a clipboard, a copy of photocopiable page 62 and a pencil.
● Explain that you want them to create a recording of everyday sounds around the school. They are then going to use these in a quiz to guess the sounds on each group's recordings.
● Tell the children that they should elect one member of the group to act as a scribe.
● Let the groups walk round the school, choosing a number of sounds to record. These could be birds singing, distant traffic, an aeroplane. The scribe should write down the name of these sounds on the photocopiable sheet as an *aide-mémoire*.
● The groups should then walk round again, taping each sound and checking that they record these in the same order as their tally sheet. Suggest that it would help to have one child saying, *Sound one, Sound two*, and so on, before each sound is recorded. Tell them that they should take note of the number the counter is on at the beginning and end of each sound. Ensure that the counters are all set to zero before they begin recording.
● Explain that when they have recorded their sounds they should play the tape back to check that the sounds have recorded successfully.
● Bring the groups back together once they have finished and give each group some paper. Ask each group in turn to play their recordings to the rest of the class. The other groups should write down what they think each sound is.
● The group who identifies the most sounds is the winner.
● After the activity, encourage the children to talk about all the different sounds that they can hear around the school. Were there any sounds that they could not recognise in the recordings? Are there any sounds that they are not aware of but that can still be heard? Perhaps some sounds are so familiar that the children don't hear them anymore.

Differentiation

More able children could use their sound tapes as a basis for inter-class quizzes. Less able children may wish to explore using a range of different sounds, such as children's voices. They could have a 'Who is speaking?' quiz.

AGE RANGE 5–11

LEARNING OBJECTIVE
To make finger puppets and use them in a role-play to encourage appropriate speaking and listening.

CURRICULUM LINKS
QCA citizenship, Unit 1: Taking part.

Problem puppets

What you need
A board and writing materials; photocopiable page 65, enough for one per group (for more durable finger puppets, plain material or strong paper could be used); felt-tipped pens; material; string or wool; glue.

What to do
● Using whole-class discussion, ask the children to list some of the common problems and issues that they face in their lives. This might include, a friend being nasty in the playground or an argument at home. Record these on the board.
● Agree on one of these problems to form the basis for a puppet show.
● With the children, decide on a short-story scenario that incorporates the chosen problem. Write the scenario on the board and talk about how the problem could be resolved. Encourage the children to think of positive solutions.
● Agree on four characters that will be involved in the puppet show and write these on the board. Talk about the different roles each character may play.
● Put the children into groups of four. Give each group a copy of photocopiable page 63 and a selection of puppet-making materials. Let them make the finger puppets. These should reflect the list of characters involved in the scenario. Encourage the children to add facial features, hair and clothes.
● Tell the children that they are going to use these puppets to act out the scenario. Encourage each group to think about what is happening in the scenario and think of a positive way to resolve the problem or issue. Each child should play a role with a puppet.
● Encourage the children to write down what each character says and does.
● When the groups have had time to practise their role plays, ask them to play their puppet dramas to the rest of the class.

Differentiation
Encourage older, or more able, children to write short-story scenarios that may be used as puppet dramas. For older groups, they could each have a different scenario to perform in front of the class. Allow younger, or less able, children to engage in conversation with the puppets. Encourage them to develop two-way dialogue between themselves and the puppets.

AGE RANGE 6–11

LEARNING OBJECTIVE
To research a subject and present the research to a group.

CURRICULUM LINKS
QCA citizenship, Unit 3: Animals and us; Unit 4: People who help us.

Fact buster!

What you need
A board and writing materials; photocopiable page 66, enough for one per child; pens; research tools, such as the school or class library, CD-ROMS, the Internet.

What to do
● Before the lesson, write a list of topics that you want the children to research on the board. The suggestions below focus on areas covered in Units 3 and 4 of the QCA Schemes of Work for Citizenship, but you could choose any relevant topics to the children's current learning. Topics could include:

1) Keeping an animal safe and happy.
2) What organisations do to help animals.
3) Ways to support your local community.
4) Duties of a community police officer.

● At the start of the lesson, tell the children you want them to undertake their own research and that they are going to prepare a short talk for the rest of the class on a chosen topic.
● Show them the list of topics you have prepared on the board, and read through them. Encourage the children to discuss what each topic is about and what kind of information they would need to research to give a talk on it.
● Give each child a copy of photocopiable page 64 and discuss it with them. Talk about the different ways of researching you want them to think about, and how to plan their talk.
● Let the children choose a topic to research and begin to fill in their sheets. This activity could take place over a period of time, so that each child has time to conduct their research, write up their findings and present their talk to the class.
● Encourage them to draw posters, diagrams and pictures to help them present information in their talks.

Differentiation
Let more able children support less able children, perhaps researching a topic together. Less able children could also prepare their talk as a group, with each member presenting a short part of the talk.

Games for Building
Social Skills
BRIGHT
IDEAS

AGE RANGE 5–11

LEARNING OBJECTIVE
To copy a sequence of movements; to respond to a partner.

CURRICULUM LINKS
QCA citizenship, Unit 1: Taking part.

Copycat

What you need
A large, clear space, such as the hall or playground.

What to do
● Organise the class into pairs and tell each pair of children to label themselves A and B.
● Tell the pairs to face each other, approximately four paces apart.
● Explain that they are going to play a game of 'Follow-my-leader. Tell them that child A is going to lead in the first instance by making slow movements (such as raising an arm, standing on one leg, or touching the ground) for child B to follow. Tell child B to follow the precise sequence of actions that child A makes.
● Give the children between ten and twenty seconds to try this.
● Then tell the children to reverse the roles and let child B lead, making movements for child A to follow.
● At this point it may be helpful to have a brief class discussion on how the children are finding the exercise. Some children are likely to say how difficult they find it to follow their partners, because the actions are unclear or too fast.
● Discuss with the children the best way to help each other to follow accurately and clearly. Explain that the leader's actions need to be slow, deliberate and clear.
● Allow the children to try again in their pairs, taking it turns to be the leader.
● When they become more confident and skilled, invite them to prepare a short movement piece, where one child mirrors the other, to perform to another pair.

Differentiation
For less able children, extend the movement sequence from the original 20 seconds to 30 seconds, and then further as confidence and ability grows. Let more able children lead a small group, making slow movements that the group should follow.

AGE RANGE 5–9

LEARNING OBJECTIVE
To verbalise feelings and recognise them in others.

CURRICULUM LINKS
QCA citizenship, Unit 1: Taking part.

Expressing feelings

What you need
A story book; photocopiable page 67, enough for one per child; a board and writing materials; pencils.

What to do
● Read a story to the class, and use it as a vehicle for asking the children to name different feelings and recognise them in others. Ask the children about the characters in the story and how they feel in different situations.
● Give each child a copy of photocopiable page 67.
● Look at the first column together. Ask the children what all the words in this column are, and confirm that they are all feelings, for example: worried, excited and happy.
● Invite the children to expand on these feelings and introduce further words that may identify the feelings more specifically. For example, worried/anxious, excited/elated, happy/contented. Write down the children's suggestions on the board.
● Some children may find it difficult to verbalise feelings. Employ photographs showing different emotions on people's faces to help them. Use these as part of the whole class's work on PSHE and citizenship.
● The second column of the photocopiable sheet lists some situations that may evoke the feelings in the first column. Look at these with the children and ask them to match the situation up to the feeling.
● Challenge the children to add to the list of situations and identify the feelings that are most likely to occur as a result. Encourage the children to discuss why these feelings are likely to arise.
● Finish, either as a whole class or in small groups, by letting the children create a small drama to illustrate a situation from the list and to verbally demonstrate a particular feeling. Encourage them to think about how to convey the feeling through their words, facial expressions and actions.

Differentiation
Let all of the children make posters or draw pictures to reinforce appropriate behaviours, and support a positive class and school ethos. More able children could create story scenarios to support the posters. Less able children could show their posters to the class and talk about these.

AGE RANGE 5–9

LEARNING OBJECTIVE
To learn about the needs of animals and how to care for them; to listen and respond to others.

CURRICULUM LINKS
QCA citizenship, Unit 1: Taking part; Unit 3: Animals and us.

What am I?

What you need
Reference books on how to care for animals; Internet access (optional); paper; pencils.

What to do
● Sit the class in a circle and place a volunteer in the middle.
● Give this child the name of an animal or pet, secretly. For example, a dog or a rabbit.
● Tell the children in the circle that they are going to take it in turns to ask questions to find out which animal the child in the middle is.
● Explain that they must listen to each other's questions carefully and the response given by the child. They may only guess which animal the child in the middle is when it is their turn.
● The children should be encouraged to ask questions that focus on how to care for animals and the importance of treating animals well. For example, *Do you need grooming? How often do you need to be fed? How much exercise do you need?*
● The child who guesses the animal correctly becomes the next person in the middle.
● As follow-up work for this activity, the children could choose an animal, perhaps a pet they have at home, and research the basic needs of that animal. Give them headings to focus their research, such as food and drink, safety, cleanliness, companionship, care when ill.

Differentiation
Less able children could draw pictures of their favourite animals and use these to contribute to a book or display on caring well for animals. More able children can create guide books on basic animal care for use by other children.

Are you cross?
Emotion cards

| Sad | Happy | Frightened |

| Irritated | Excited | Furious |

| Joyful | Upset | Amused |

| Cross | Nervous | Friendly |

Games for Building
Social Skills
BRIGHT
IDEAS

Are you cross?

Guess the sound

Sound recorded	Counter number
	From To

Puppets

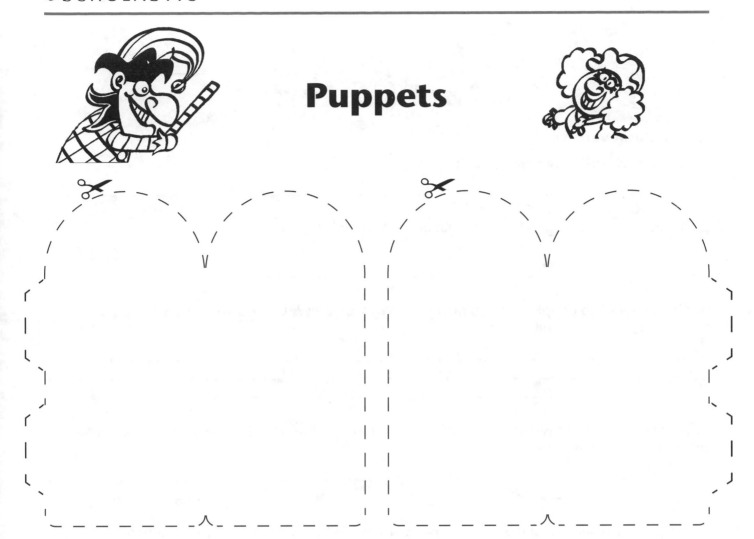

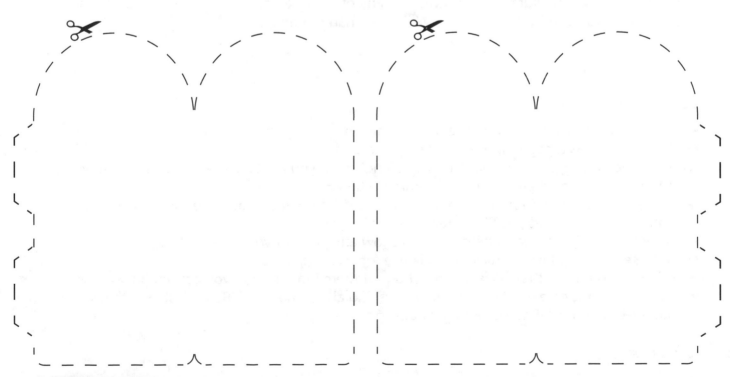

Fact buster!

Researching your topic

1. Name of chosen topic for research

_____

2. Where are you going to find information on this topic?

_____

_____

3. Think about the people that can help you. Who are they? Do you know how to contact them? If not, ask an adult to help you.

_____

_____

_____

4. Some organisations will send you information through the post. List any organisations you think might be able to help you.

_____

_____

5. Is it possible that you could invite someone from the local community to the school to talk about their work? Who might this be?

_____

_____

6. Check with other children in the class. Are any of them researching the same topic? If so, then perhaps you can help each other. Write their names here.

_____

_____

Planning your talk

- Plan out your talk when you have all your information together.
- A good talk has a beginning, a middle and an end.
- At the beginning of your talk, tell the audience what you are talking about. Tell them why you chose this topic and where you got your information.
- In the middle, or main part, of your talk, give the information you have found. Was any information a surprise to you? If so, tell your audience.
- Some people get bored quite quickly, so show any pictures you have found.
- At the end of the talk, thank your audience for listening to you.
- Ask the audience if they have any questions. If there is a question you cannot answer, do not worry, you cannot be expected to know everything about the topic. Be honest. Say that you do not know, but you will find out and get back to them.

Good luck!

Games for Building Social Skills **BRIGHT IDEAS**

Expressing feelings

● Match the situation with the most likely feeling. Then add some of your own suggestions.

Cross	You've no one to play with.
Happy	It's the school holidays.
Upset	Your best friend won't be your best friend any more.
Excited	Your teacher's cross with you.
Scared	You're being bullied.
Nervous	You're going on holiday.
Lonely	Returning to school after the holidays.
Worried	You've had an argument.

CHAPTER 5

Small group participation

AGE RANGE 9–11

LEARNING OBJECTIVE
To work as a member of a team; to manage losing appropriately.

CURRICULUM LINKS
QCA citizenship, Unit 1: Taking part.

Give, take or swap

What you need
Card copies of photocopiable page 76 (enough for one between four children); card copies of photocopiable page 77, cut up into cards (enough for one set of cards per pair); dice; coloured counters; felt-tipped pens.

What to do
● Split the class into pairs. Explain that they are in their teams and are going to play a board game against another team. Let each team choose another team to play against.
● Give each group of four players a copy of photocopiable page 76, and each team a set of 'Give, take or swap cards' from photocopiable page 77 and some felt-tipped pens.
● Before the start of the game, ask each team to choose a colour and mark the gameboard with 15 squares of that colour. Each team should take it in turns to mark a square. Stress that they must not mark the 'Start' or 'Finish' squares.
● Tell the children that the idea of the game is to get rid of as many 'Give, take or swap' cards as they can.
● Explain that teams turn their cards face down and take it in turns to throw the die. When team A lands on one of team B's coloured squares, team B takes one of team A's cards. If the instruction on the card is 'Give' they benefit from giving team A one of their cards, if the instruction is 'Take' then team B must take one of team A's cards and if the instruction is 'Swap' team B has to swap a card with team A.

● Explain that the first team to reach the 'Finish' square stops the game and the winners are those with the fewest cards left.

Differentiation
Those players who play the game fluently may introduce penalties and bonuses to increase the game's complexity. Less able children may find it easier to reduce the number of coloured squares marked on the gameboard, and only have one of each 'Give, take or swap' cards.

Games for Building
Social Skills

AGE RANGE 7–11

LEARNING OBJECTIVE
To work together to create a simple musical piece to play.

CURRICULUM LINKS
QCA citizenship, Unit 1: Taking part.

Musical challenge

What you need
A variety of tuned and untuned musical instruments; a quiet area to work.

What to do
● Put the class into groups of four. Explain that you want each group to create a musical piece that all members of the group will contribute to.
● Tell the groups that there should be parts of the musical piece where all members of the group play together, and other parts where one or two members play while the remainder of the group listen.
● Give each group a selection of tuned and untuned instruments, and set a time limit for them to create their piece.
● Encourage the children in the groups to explore the instruments and to think about how the different sounds can be played together.
● Invite them to experiment with the different ways instruments, such as tambourines and cymbals, can be played.

● Tell the groups, as they are practising their piece, that they should also give the piece a name or title. To create a sense of unity to the groups, the children could compose a piece of music that relates to a particular theme, such as summer, holidays or the jungle.

● At the end of the time, ask each group to play their finished piece to the rest of the class.

Differentiation
More able children can tape-record their music and challenge another group to recreate the piece after listening to the tape several times. They could also use a form of notation and write down the music. Encourage less able children to distinguish the sounds made by the different instruments.

AGE RANGE 6–11

LEARNING OBJECTIVE
To work with others to present dramas based on areas of citizenship to younger children.

CURRICULUM LINKS
QCA citizenship, Unit 1: Taking part.

Puppet Show

What you need
A board and writing materials; photocopiable page 65 (enough for the children to work in groups of two or three); thin card or material and tracing paper; felt-tipped pens.

What to do
● Before the lesson, write a list of themes that you would like the children to base a puppet show on the board. Themes such as 'Getting lost' or 'Don't smash windows!' focus on Units 4 and 9, respectively, of the QCA Schemes of Work for Citizenship, but you may wish to link this in to current work the children are doing. You could also use the dilemmas in chapter 3 of this book.

● At the start of the lesson, put the class into groups of two or three, and give each group a copy of photocopiable page 65. (Have additional copies available in case groups want to use more puppets in their drama.)

● Explain to the children that you want them to choose a theme from those given, or choose a theme themselves, and create a puppet show in their groups.

● When the group has chosen its theme, tell the children to make up their puppets according to the characters they want to include in their drama. They can make paper puppets or copy the outlines on the photocopiable page onto the card. They can also create material puppets by tracing the outlines using tracing paper, placing the paper onto the material, and cutting along the lines.

● Then they can create a puppet show based on their chosen theme.

● When the groups have had time to practise their puppet show, they can present it to their peers first. Ask the rest of the class to assess the puppet shows.

● Let the groups go back and modify their puppet shows to raise the standards of performance.

● They can then perform the puppet shows to younger children. Presenting key areas of the citizenship curriculum to younger children will reinforce appropriate behaviours for all involved.

● It is helpful if the children engage in active discussion with their audience following the performances to reinforce the key elements of their chosen themes.

Differentiation
Less able children may like to create their own style of puppet using other materials, or using their own templates. Older, or more able, children could work with younger ones to assist them in performing their own puppet shows.

AGE RANGE 5–6

LEARNING OBJECTIVE
To work as a member of a group to complete a given model, and to use rules to support the process.

CURRICULUM LINKS
QCA citizenship, Unit 1: Taking part.

Build and snap

What you need
Packs of 'Snap cards'; LEGO bricks, or other construction materials; dice (enough of each resource for the children to work in groups of four); copies of photocopiable page 78, copied on to card and cut up.

What to do
● Put the class into pairs and ask them to team up with another pair.
● Give each group of four children a pack of 'Snap Cards', a die and a selection of LEGO bricks.
● Explain to the children that they are going to play 'Snap', and remind them how to play this if necessary. Tell them that when 'snap' is achieved the winner should take the cards on the pile as normal.
● When the winner has taken the cards, they then throw the die. If a 6 is thrown, for example, the team take six LEGO bricks. If a 4 is thrown, then four LEGO bricks are taken, and so on.
● Let the children start to play the game, and give them a set amount of time – around five to ten minutes.
● At the end of the given time, each pair will have accumulated a number of LEGO bricks.
● Place the cards from photocopiable page 78 face down on a table. Invite each team to come and take one.
● Explain that each team must build the model stated on their card with the bricks they have collected.
● When the children have built their models, judge who has built the best model. They are the winners.

Differentiation
Less able children could be given tasks, such as building a bridge with 70 LEGO bricks, as a separate activity to get them used to such restrictions. More able children can be introduced to more complex instructions and asked to build items using more restrictions.

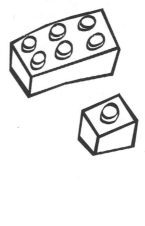

AGE RANGE 7–11

LEARNING OBJECTIVE
To play a game that requires speed and concentration against others; to use rules appropriately; to manage winning and losing appropriately.

CURRICULUM LINKS
QCA citizenship, Unit 7: Children's rights; Unit 8: How do rules and laws affect me?

Twist

What you need
A pack of ordinary playing cards (enough for the children to work in groups of four).

What to do
● Put the class into groups of four and give each group a pack of playing cards.
● Ask each group to nominate a dealer, and ask all the dealers to give ten cards out to each player. Tell the children that these cards should be placed face up on the table in front of them.
● Tell the dealers to place the remaining cards in the middle of the table, face down.
● Explain how to play the game to the children:
● The top card on the middle pile should be turned over so that the players can see it.
● The four players should look at their own cards. If any player has the next number to the card on the middle pile, in any suit, that player should put it on top of the card in the middle. For example, if the five of clubs is the card on the middle pile and a player has a four (of any suit), they would place this on top of the five of clubs. Then another player may put down a three and a two (of any suit).
● Players are only allowed to use one hand to put cards on the middle pile, and they should do so as quickly as possible before another player puts a card there.
● If no player can put a card down, the group should call out *Twist*. The top card on the middle pile can then be put to the bottom of the pile and the next card on the pile turned over. The players then continue.
● If a player calls out *Twist* in the wrong place, that player pays a penalty and has to take an extra card from the middle.
● The player who succeeds in getting rid of all their cards first is the winner.
● Let the children play the game. To play a second game, the cards must be really well shuffled.

Differentiation
With more able children, let them try playing with two packs of cards. Less able children may be introduced to the playing cards and asked to make suits, starting with the Ace and working through to the King. This will familiarise them with the different cards.

Games for Building
Social Skills

BRIGHT
IDEAS

AGE RANGE 7–8

LEARNING OBJECTIVE
To work with others to create a strategy and overcome problems.

CURRICULUM LINKS
QCA citizenship, Unit 1: Taking part; Unit 3: Animals and us.

Car mad

What you need
Car mats; toy vehicles; photocopiable page 79, copied on to card and cut up; photocopiable page 80 (enough of each resource for the children to work in groups of three or four).

What to do
● Put the class into groups of three or four.
● Give each group a car mat, toy vehicles and the cut-out pictures from photocopiable page 79.
● Ask the children to set up a town on the car mat, placing the pictures of buildings onto it. The children may also add their own buildings.
● Give the groups one of the scenarios from photocopiable page 79 (but not the solutions). Read the scenario to the groups if necessary, or tape-record the scenarios so that the children can replay them should they need to.
● Explain to the children that they must overcome the challenges described in the scenario by creating an appropriate strategy in their groups.
● The children can act out the scenario using the car mat and vehicles. Encourage them to set up the scene outlined in the scenario. For example, in Scenario 1 they could place the school on the mat and mark the roadworks.
● Encourage the children to try out their ideas to see if they will work.
● After a set amount of time, ask the groups to share their ideas with another group.
● Then read out the solutions from the photocopiable page. Let the groups try these out if they are new ideas.
● Invite the groups to share solutions that are not on your list. Ask the groups to agree which is the best solution and discuss why they think it is the best.
● Follow the same procedure for the next scenario.

Differentiation
For more able children, make the problems increasingly complex, perhaps giving one problem and then making it more challenging by adding a secondary problem. Less able children can be encouraged to verbalise the scenario to make sure that they understand it and also understand the problems. An adult may support the group when they have trialled their solutions to ensure the children have explored the challenge fully.

AGE RANGE 7–11

LEARNING OBJECTIVE
To respond to instructions and work as a team; to use effective listening.

CURRICULUM LINKS
QCA citizenship, Unit 1: Taking part; Unit 8: How do rules and laws affect me?

Move it!

What you need
A number of copies of photocopiable page 81, copied on to card and cut up; space for the children to run a short distance, such as the hall.

What to do
● Before the lesson, arrange the instructions from photocopiable page 81 in piles of four, in a line, at one end of the hall or the area you are using.
● At the start of the lesson, put the class into teams of four.
● Instruct the teams to sit at the opposite end of the hall, facing the cards, in a line. Explain that their instructions are placed opposite them, and make sure they can all see the cards.
● On the start signal, Player 1 should run across the room to the list of instructions, read it silently, put it at the bottom of the pile and run back to Player 2.

● Player 1 should then give Player 2 the instructions verbally and go to the back of the team. Player 2 must obey the instructions, which might be, *Hop back to get the next instructions.*
● When Player 2 reaches the opposite side of the room, they must read the next set of instructions silently, place them at the bottom of the instruction pile and run back to Player 3.
● Player 2 should then give Player 3 the instructions verbally and go to the back of the team.
● The teams should continue in this way, until every player has had a turn, ending with Player 1 carrying out the instructions.
● When Player 1 returns to their team, the team should all sit down. The first team to sit down is the winner.

Differentiation
More able children could make up their own instructions for the game. Less able children may need assistance with reading the instructions. Use a good reader to act as extra support for these children.

Games for Building
Social Skills
BRIGHT IDEAS

AGE RANGE 7–8

LEARNING OBJECTIVE
To listen and respond appropriately to others.

CURRICULUM LINKS
QCA citizenship, Unit 1: Taking part.

Adders

What you need
A large, clear space.

What to do
● Start with a small group of perhaps six to eight children, and ask them to stand in a circle. Tell the rest of the class to watch carefully.
● Nominate a child to stand in the middle of the circle (child A). Ask them to point to a child in the circle, child B.
● Child B must give one fact about child A. For example, *You are wearing a blue sweatshirt.*
● The child standing next to child B in the circle, child C, repeats, *You are wearing a blue sweatshirt* and adds another fact about child A. For example, *You are wearing a blue sweatshirt and you have brown hair.*
● The children should continue in a clockwise direction to repeat the facts and add one of their own until each child in the circle has had a turn. How many facts can the children remember?
● At the end of the activity, discuss ideas to help the children to retain facts. Bring the rest of the class in on the discussion and ask them to share their ideas.
● The size of the group can be increased as the children become more skilled at the activity. Or you could start the activity again with the whole class split into groups of six to eight.

Differentiation
With less able children, undertake preparatory activities to assist them in retaining facts. This might include one child stating a given number of facts about another child, thus supporting powers of observation. Let less able children join in the activity after watching it trialled a number of times. More able children may be given a minimum number of facts that they must retain, for example, seven. Let the team build to repeating seven facts, but if a child fails to remember this number they sit out. The last child to remember seven facts is the winner.

📖SCHOLASTIC

 # Give, take or swap

1 START	2	3	4	5
10●	9	8	7	6
11	12	13	14	15
20●	19	18	17	16
21	22	23	24	25
30●	29	28	27	26
31	32	33	34	35
40● FINISH	39	38	37	36

Games for Building
Social Skills **BRIGHT IDEAS**

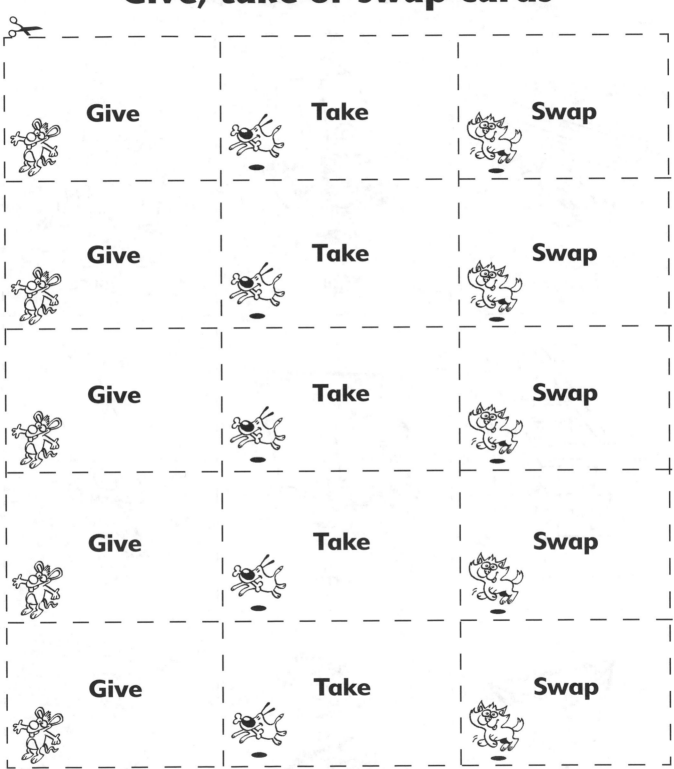

Give, take or swap cards

Give	Take	Swap
Give	Take	Swap
Give	Take	Swap
Give	Take	Swap
Give	Take	Swap

Build and snap

Bridge

Car

House

Stairs

Lorry

Boat

Three-sided shape

Stairs

Wall

Games for Building
Social Skills **BRIGHT
IDEAS**

Car mad

Fire station

Police station

Hospital

Shops

School

Play park

Library

Garage

Pedestrian crossing

Traffic lights

Car mad: scenarios

✂ -

● **Scenario 1**

The local school has written to all parents. Due to major roadworks the main road to the school will be closed to all traffic. Parents are asked to find a different way of bringing their children to the school.

   There is only one other way to the school, and this is across a very, very busy dual carriageway. Can you help to solve the problem and get the children to the school?

● Possible solutions:

1. Build a bridge over the dual carriageway for the children and parents to walk across.
2. Open a car park in a nearby field and have a 'walking bus' from there every morning.
3. Get a bus stop put near to the roadworks and not too far from the school, so people can use the bus.

L -

✂ -

● **Scenario 2**

You have just heard on your police radio that there is a driver driving madly in the area and is about to reach the road you're in. You have been asked to shut off the road and to stop the car before someone gets injured. Unfortunately, the reason you're in that road is because there is a party of 30 school children out on a trip. It sounds like they're coming along just at the time when the mad driver is going to be in that road.

   Agree which member of your group will act as the 'mad driver'.
Before you act this part out, consider all the options. What will you do?

● Possible solutions:

1. Stop the children, then wait for the driver to come down the road, follow him and try to stop him.
2. Use your radio to find out where the car is and place your colleagues along those roads.
3. Place road blocks along the road.

L -

Move it!

Hop back to get the next instructions.

Run back to the instructions, turning round three times before you reach them.

Skip back to the instructions and jump up high four times before reaching them.

Jump back to the instructions and read them in reverse order (from the last word to the first word).

Run sideways like a crab all the way to the instructions.

Hop, skip and jump back to the instructions.

Runs as fast as you can to the instructions, but you're only allowed to whisper the next instructions to your team member.

Crawl on all fours to the instructions.

CHAPTER 6

Diversity

AGE RANGE 6–11

LEARNING OBJECTIVE
To recognise that everyone is physically different, and to discuss and celebrate differences.

CURRICULUM LINKS
QCA citizenship, Unit 1: Taking part; Unit 5: Living in a diverse world.

Silhouettes

What you need
An overhead projector; a plain wall; a chair; flip-chart paper; pencils; sticky tack.

What to do
● Before the lesson, place the overhead projector about one metre from the plain wall and switch it on. Focus the light on to the wall, maintaining a small area of light large enough to create a silhouette of a child's head and shoulders.
● Stick a piece of flip-chart paper in the lit area, fixing it securely with sticky tack. (This needs to be secure enough to allow a pencil to move over it and at a height to capture the silhouette of a child's head and shoulders.)
● Place the chair sideways-on between the overhead projector and the paper.
● At the beginning of the lesson, put the children in pairs and ask for a volunteer pair. Put child A in position on the chair before switching on the overhead projector. Point out to the children that they must not look directly at the overhead projector light.

● Readjust the equipment if necessary to ensure that child A's outline features are captured on the paper on the wall. Give child B a pencil and ask them to draw around the silhouette they can see on the paper, focusing on every small detail of the facial and hair features. Encourage child A to remain perfectly still while the drawing is in progress.
● Once the silhouette is completed, ask child B to stand back and check their work before child A moves from the chair. Do the rest of the class think that all the details have been drawn?
● Let the pair repeat the process, with child A drawing around child B's silhouette.
● Show the class the two drawings. Can they guess who is who? Is it easy to recognise each child from their silhouettes? If so, why? Suggest they look closely at physical differences, such as nose shapes, hair styles, and so on.
● Extended the discussion to encourage the children to consider appropriate and positive ways to describe their peers. So, for example, if one child is very tall or short, the children will celebrate the benefits of these attributes.

Differentiation
Less able children may find it challenging to create a defined silhouette, so let them draw round a hand or foot first. More able children could set up the activity from scratch, arranging the overhead projector and ensuring everything is in the best position to achieve a well-defined and accurate silhouette.

AGE RANGE 5–6

LEARNING OBJECTIVE
To encourage the children to recognise, accept and celebrate physical differences in each other.

CURRICULUM LINKS
QCA citizenship, Unit 1: Taking part; Unit 5: Living in a diverse world.

I'm special

What you need
A board and writing materials; A3 paper for drawing; drawing equipment, such as pencils, pastels, coloured pencils, wax crayons.

What to do
● Discuss with the class the common physical features that we all have. Make a list of the things the children suggest, such as a mouth, two eyes, ten fingers and toes.
● Use the discussion to highlight the differences too. Ask the children to suggest what is different about each of them physically. They may suggest the colour of their eyes, their face shape, or skin colour. List these on the board.
● Put the children into pairs. Give each child paper and drawing equipment and invite them to draw their partner, asking them to capture the physical differences where possible.
● When the whole class have completed their pictures, display them on the wall. Are the children able to identify each other from the pictures? If so, how can they tell which picture is of which child? They may use identifying features, such as hair styles, glasses or skin colour.
● Using the pictures, highlight features that are common to groups of children. For example, eye, skin and hair colour.

● Encourage the children to celebrate differences in physical appearance. This might include recognising the benefits of having long, braided or short hair for example. Encouraging open, positive discussion demystifies that which is different.

Differentiation
Less able children could draw two pictures – one of themselves and the second of a child who looks different from them. Encourage them to draw differences between the two pictures, for example: *I have black hair, the child in the second picture has blond hair; I have black skin, the child in the second drawing has white skin.* More able children should be encouraged to consider features beyond that of physical appearance and consider what traits make people like or dislike a person (that they are good tempered, friendly, helpful).

AGE RANGE 7–11

LEARNING OBJECTIVE
To recognise and accept that we react and respond differently to situations that make us angry.

CURRICULUM LINKS
QCA citizenship, Unit 1: Taking part; Unit 5: Living in a diverse world.

You make me cross!

What you need
A prepared role-play scenario.

What to do
● Tell the children you want them to perform a role-play. Put them into groups of four and tell them the scenario:

You are at home. Your older sister is being particularly mean to you. She has taken your last few sweets. What do you do?

● Explain that two children from each group should act out the role-play while the other two watch.
● Go around the groups and help the children to role-play getting angry or losing their temper with their 'older sister'. Ask all four children in the group to share how this makes them feel. Discuss whether there is another way that the matter might be resolved.
● Invite the children within their groups to share opinions as to why some children do seem to get angry or lose their temper, and why others do not. Encourage the groups to share ideas on how to support a classmate who has a temper or gets angry. Deliberately confining the activity to a small number of children allows opportunity for in-depth discussion.
● As a class, discuss the different ways that the children react and respond when they are angry. For example, crying, running to their rooms, hitting someone. Discuss positive way of managing anger and destructive ways too.
● Discuss simple problems that the children might face on a regular basis. Focus on scenarios that may lead to the children becoming angry or losing their temper and discuss ways of managing their behaviour.

Differentiation
Encourage less able children to repeatedly role-play appropriate ways to manage anger. For those children who are more able and also positive in the way they do manage their anger, encourage them to investigate other areas of their personality in the same ways. For example, feeling down or upset, or being scared.

AGE RANGE 7–11

LEARNING OBJECTIVE
To understand some of the challenges faced by people who live in extreme conditions.

CURRICULUM LINKS
QCA citizenship, Unit 1: Taking part; Unit 5: Living in a diverse world.

Hot and cold

What you need
A4 paper; cut-out word cards from photocopiable page 92 (enough for groups of six children); reference books about hot and cold countries.

What to do
● In advance of the lesson, create a set of questions to encourage discussion about living in places that have extreme temperatures.
● Questions might include:

1) Is it always very hot in hot countries – night and day?
2) Do very hot or cold countries encounter seasons as we do?
3) What modes of transport are used in hot or cold countries?
4) What extra problems might residents face? (Car radiators overheating or freezing.)
5) Which materials are likely to be used, or not used, and why? (Tarmac will not be used in very hot regions as it will melt in the heat.)

● At the start of the lesson, put the children into groups of six and ask each group to sit at a table. Give each group a set of the cut-out word cards.
● Ask the groups to think about which of the things on the word cards might be found in hot or cold places. Tell the groups they should sort the words into two separate groups – hot and cold. Explain that some are easier than others, and some might apply to both hot and cold places.
● When the groups have finished, compare the sorted word cards and begin a class discussion on what it might be like to live in places of extreme temperature. Use your prepared questions to stimulate the discussion.
● Only introduce reference books after the discussion as an aid to answer any questions that the children may have been unable to answer.
● Encourage the children to outline what they have learned. Are the class able to provide six facts that they did not know before about the challenges facing people who live in a very different climate to themselves?

Differentiation
More able children could create their own sets of questions to use and ask other children for the answers. Less able children may draw pictures to illustrate the challenges faced in hot and cold climates.

AGE RANGE 5–11

LEARNING OBJECTIVE
To gain insight and understanding about the
challenges that some people face in everyday life.

CURRICULUM LINKS
QCA citizenship, Unit 1: Taking part; Unit 5: Living in
a diverse world.

Challenge

What you need

A board and writing materials; resources to disable the children, such
as blindfolds, ear defenders, small walking sticks; the resources you
will need for the activities you devise; timers that record seconds
and minutes (for use with Key Stage 2 children only, egg timers
(for Key Stage 1 children); paper; pens.

What to do

● Before the lesson, devise a series of simple activities
appropriate to your class. These might be drawing an animal
or building a simple model wall using bricks. Write these on
the board.

● In the lesson, ask the children to give you some examples
of the disabilities or handicaps that people may have, and
list these on the board. These might include, deafness, sight
impairment or blindness.

● For each of the disabilities and handicaps that the children
identified, ask them to consider the challenges that these may create
for people in everyday life. For example, challenges for blind people
when going out to the shops.

● Tell the children that they are going to try out different activities, first using all their
faculties and senses and then with a handicap. Show them the resources they can use
to give them a handicap. Can they suggest any other ways of making the activity more
difficult for themselves? They may suggest only using one hand or hopping.

● Put the class into pairs and ask them to label themselves A and B. Give each child a
timer and tell them they will time each activity that their partner does.

● Then show the children the activities on the board and make sure they know what
to do. Give them the resources they will need and set all the pairs off, telling child B to
complete each activity twice – once with full use of all faculties and senses, and
the second time with restricted use of them. After each activity, tell the
children to record what they did, what handicap they used and how
long it took.

● After a while ask the children to swap roles so that child A
completes the activities and child B records the time taken.

● Bring the children together and discuss how much longer
the activities took when the children did not have full use
of their abilities. Discuss the challenges that people with
disabilities face.

Differentiation

More able children could design an artefact that would make
life easier for someone with a disability. Less able children may
create pictures showing some of the hazards that people with a
given disability face every day.

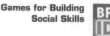

AGE RANGE 5–6

LEARNING OBJECTIVE
To describe feelings and consider how those who live differently from us may feel.

CURRICULUM LINKS
QCA citizenship, Unit 1: Taking part; Unit 5: Living in a diverse world.

Make the face

What you need
A board and writing materials; copies of photocopiable page 93 copied on to card and cut up (you need enough cards for one per child); A3 drawing or painting paper; art equipment, such as pencils, crayons, coloured pencils, paint, paintbrushes.

What to do
● Place the words cards from photocopiable page 93 face down in a pile at the front of the class.
● Ask the children to tell you the names of some feelings. For example, happy, sad and frightened. List these on the board.
● Invite the children to take it in turns to come to the front of the class and choose one of the word cards.
● Ask them to try to look or act in the way the feeling on the card suggests. Ask the class to guess which feeling the child is acting.
● Repeat this activity for a few more word cards to focus the children on the theme of expressing particular feelings.
● Ask the children how they can tell which feelings are being conveyed. For example, they might consider facial expressions and body language.
● Then give the children paper and art equipment. Give each child a word card and ask them to draw or paint what makes them feel the way the card suggests.
● Discuss each child's picture with them. Encourage the children to use a greater range of words to describe what their pictures are about.

Differentiation
Less able children could draw themselves looking the way the card suggests, such as lonely or angry, if they find drawing what makes them feel this way difficult. More able children could use newspapers as sources of information to find situations that match the feeling on their cards.

AGE RANGE 6–11

LEARNING OBJECTIVE
To investigate and consider the difficulties that people with disabilities face when living their daily lives.

CURRICULUM LINKS
QCA citizenship, Unit 5: Living in a diverse world; Unit 8: How do rules and laws affect me?

Which route shall I take?

What you need
Copies of photocopiable page 94 copied on to card and cut up; photocopiable page 95 copied on to card, enough for the children to work in pairs; dice; counters.

What to do
● Show the children the cards from photocopiable page 94. Talk through the different types of transport or mobility aids and make sure the children know what each card shows. Talk about the different types of disabilities that people may have which mean they need to use special transport or mobility aids.
● Tell the children they are going to play a board game. Put them into pairs and give each pair a gameboard (photocopiable page 95).
● Explain the rules of the game. Each child chooses an unseen transport card and assumes that type of transport or mobility aid. The children each have a counter and take it in turns to throw the die. They progress along the board until they reach an obstacle. If they are unable to move over the obstacle due to their mode of transport or mobility aid, that child misses a turn. On the next turn, the obstacle is considered to have been moved and they can pass by it.
● The first child to reach the finish wins the game.
● Go around the pairs as the children play and ask them to say how they will tackle each obstacle that they meet.
● When the children have finished playing, bring the class back together and discuss how the mobility aids or modes of transport affected their ability to move freely over the obstacles. Point out how some people have to face overcoming such difficulties in their everyday lives.

Differentiation
More able children may include their own problems and challenges into the game – whilst keeping it realistic. Less able children could work their way through a number of transport cards and feed back the challenges to an adult.

Games for Building
Social Skills **BRIGHT IDEAS**

AGE RANGE 5–7

LEARNING OBJECTIVE
To use one particular sense and discuss the challenges facing those with impaired vision.

CURRICULUM LINKS
QCA citizenship, Unit 1: Taking part; Unit 5: Living in a diverse world.

Can you guess?

What you need
A variety of different bags made from different materials, such as a paper bag, a carrier bag, a string bag, and also have two bags made from the same material but with different colours or patterns; a number of different articles, such as a hairbrush and an orange, and some articles that are the same but that differ in colour; a blindfold.

What to do
● Show all the children the different bags and ask them to name each one as you hold it up.
● Ask for a volunteer to come up and be blindfolded.
● Tell the rest of the class to watch carefully as you choose one of the bags. Then choose a number of different articles to place in the bag, letting the children see you do this.
● Let the child with the blindfold feel the bag and ask them to identify which bag has been chosen from the selection by touch alone. Guide them if necessary, by suggesting they think about the texture of the bag.
● Then ask the child to pick out one article at a time from the bag and, by touch alone, say what each article is.
● Repeat the sequence, blindfolding another child. This time, choose a bag that is made from the same material as another bag and is only different in pattern or colour. Place articles in the bag that give a similar challenge, such as two bricks that are the same apart from their colour.
● Can the children say why it was more difficult for this child to identify the bag and the objects? Try to encourage the children to appreciate the challenges for people who are blind. Highlight how it is possible to tell the difference between different materials by touch, but it is not possible to identify colour or pattern this way. Focus on feelings as well as the challenge that this presents. Ask, *How do you think it feels not being able to see? Do you think it would be difficult to complete some tasks?*

Differentiation
More able children may like to write a list of questions to ask a blind person about their life. Less able children could wear a blindfold and experience 'blindness' for a period of time, such as playtime, and then feed back to the class on the greatest challenges they faced. They must be carefully supervised.

AGE RANGE 7–11

LEARNING OBJECTIVE
To highlight diversity problems through role-play and ask the children to come up with solutions.

CURRICULUM LINKS
QCA citizenship, Unit 1: Taking part; Unit 5: Living in a diverse world.

Help

What you need
Copies of the scenarios on photocopiable page 96, cut out and enough for each group; space for the children to role-play the scenarios.

What to do
● Tell the children they are going to investigate difficult situations that they may face in their own lives, or that other people may face, through role-play.

● Put the class into groups of four to six children. Give each group a scenario from photocopiable page 96 to analyse. Explain that in each group the children must allocate the parts involved in their role-play.

● Let the children discuss their scenario for five minutes and then tell them to practise the role-play.

● Encourage them to think carefully about the problem and about how they would feel or how they would help a person in that situation. Invite them to find a positive solution to the problem.

● Ask each group to take it in turns to role-play their scene in front of the rest of the class.

● When they have finished, ask the children watching to guess what problem the drama has highlighted.

● Discussion after each role-play is important. Focus on the feelings of each character. Look at different ways in which the problem could have been solved. Consider how the characters might be supported, by friends, teachers or any other group. For instance, using the scenario in which Hanif is constantly picked on by other children because of the colour of his skin, consider the following: How does Hanif feel? Have any of the children any experience of being picked on because of physical features? Why do the children think those who are picking on Hanif do it?

● The children may draw pictures of either one of the problems listed or choose another similar situation, perhaps something that has happened to them or something they have witnessed. The content of the picture can be shared with the class. The pictures can also be used as a stimulus to prepare a class assembly.

Differentiation
More able children could undertake a survey amongst other classes or year groups to investigate incidents of bullying and the reasons that these have happened. This could lead to further work on managing diversity more positively in the school. Less able children can create posters as part of a display entitled, 'We're all different – isn't it great!'

AGE RANGE 7–11

LEARNING OBJECTIVE
To consider different lifestyles; to consider the differences and challenges faced by people in the type of dwelling they live in and how this might affect their lives.

CURRICULUM LINKS
QCA citizenship, Unit 5: Living in a diverse world.

I live here

What you need
A board and writing materials; drawing and painting materials; sheets of A3 paper.

What to do
● Introduce the activity with a short discussion about the different types of dwellings that people live in. For example, a travelling caravan, a bungalow, a detached house, a bed and breakfast, a seventh floor flat, a terraced house, a ground-floor flat. List these on the board.

● Talk about the similar and different features of these dwellings. Which ones would the children like to live in? Which ones would they not want to live in? What are their reasons?
● Ask the children to either draw the type of dwelling they live in, or to draw one of the types of dwellings from the list (be sensitive to any children in the class who may not have a conventional home).
● Invite the children to talk about what they need from their homes.
● Write a list of people who have different needs from their homes on the board. For example, a fit elderly person, an elderly person who has difficulty walking, a parent with a baby in a pram, a family with four children, a lady in a wheelchair.
● Ask the children to compare this list with the list of dwellings.
● Encourage the children to think about the challenges different people may face in each dwelling and whether they can be overcome. For example, an elderly person with difficulty walking who lives in a seventh floor flat will be fine within the flat but will only be able to access it if the lifts are always working.
● Ask the children to consider which type of home might be best suited to each of the people? Why? Ask them to compile a list of needs that each person on the board may have and to design the ideal home for one of them.
● The children can, as an extension activity, research who has responsibilities for helping those who need housing. They can choose to be one of the people on the prepared list – with specific needs – and write a letter outlining the difficulties they face, and the type of housing that would assist them.

Differentiation
More able children could design and make a book about the different ways people live in their own community, and the challenges that some children face. Less able children can create pictures for the book.

Hot and cold

Mountains	Skis
Sand	Thermal clothing
Ice	Hot food
Glaciers	Freezer
No water	Roofed buildings
Flat landscape	Scrubland
Hats	Fruit trees
Fires	Ice-cold drinks

Games for Building Social Skills

BRIGHT IDEAS

Make the face

Afraid	Scared	Tired
Happy	Sad	Worried
Upset	Bored	Disgusted
Lonely	Angry	Sorry
Embarrassed	Shocked	Nervous

Route cards

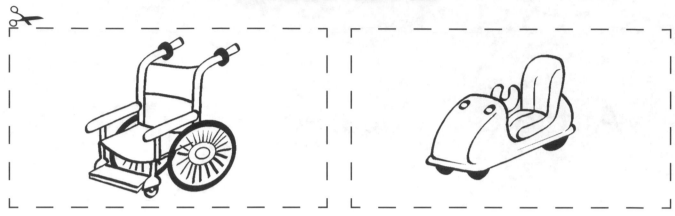

Games for Building
Social Skills

BRIGHT
IDEAS

Which route shall I take?

1 START	2	3	4	5
10	9	8	7	6
11	12	13	14	15
20	19	18	17	16
21	22	23	24	25
30	29	28	27	26
31	32	33	34	35
40 FINISH	39	38	37	36

Help

Hanif is constantly picked on by other children because of the colour of his skin.

Sami has a long-term medical problem and this means he has to use a wheelchair. He has no one to play with at school or at home.

One of the children that lives near you keeps inviting you round to play. You don't want to go because his mum is weird – seriously weird! Your mum says she has mental health problems.

Due to an accident when she was small, Amy has a major disfigurement on her face. She gets picked on by some of the older children.

Josh is five years old. He has had an accident and his arm is in plaster. He isn't allowed to run around with the other children in the playground. Some of the other children are calling him names.

Emmanuel is in foster care. He is new to the school and is finding it very hard to adjust to the foster home and the school. It doesn't help that some of his classmates make nasty comments about his family. In particular they make rude comments about his mother being unable to look after him.

Games for Building Social Skills **BRIGHT IDEAS**